Collins Canadian Wor[ld]

D1365699

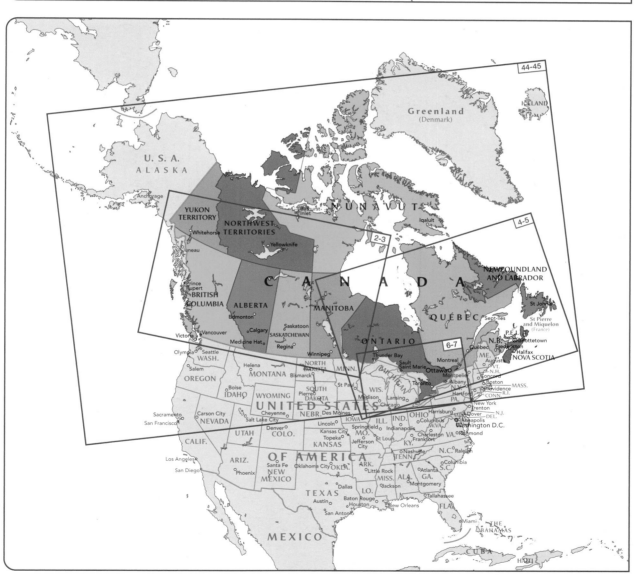

Collins

Canada
Western Canada

Conic Equidistant Projection

4   1:7 000 000

Canada

Eastern Canada

Conic Equidistant Projection

1:3 500 000

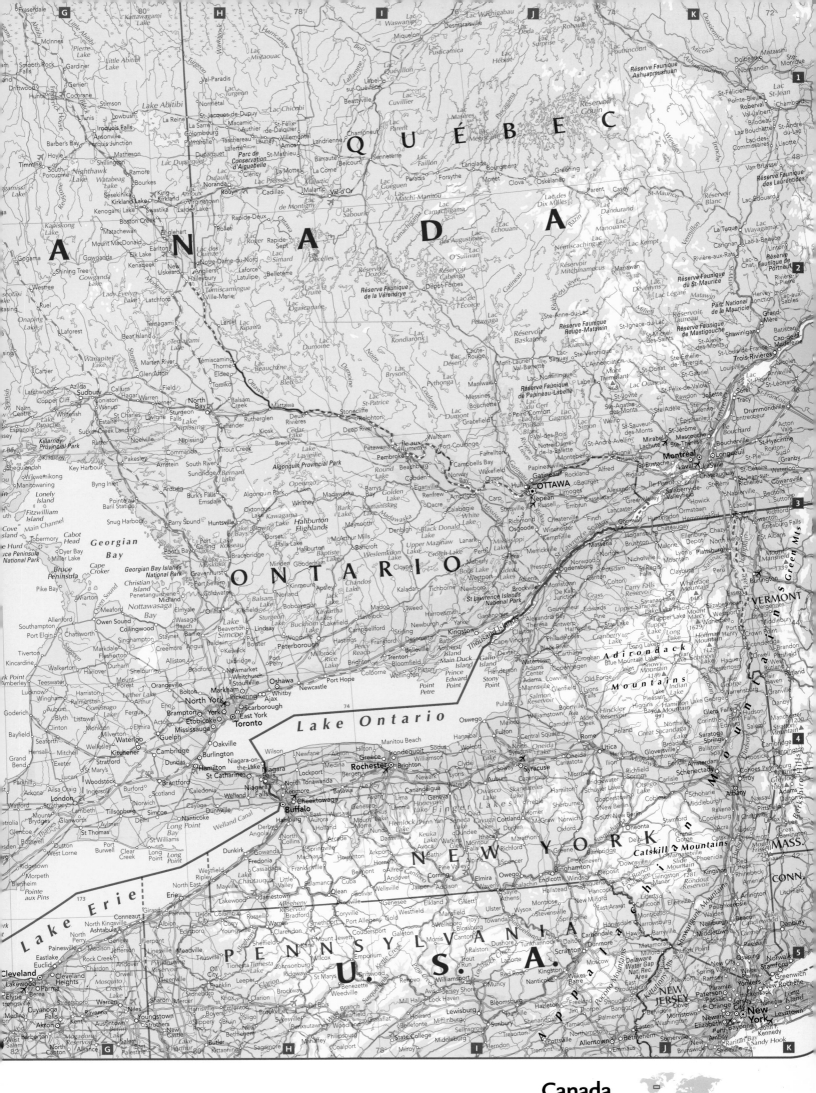

Canada
Great Lakes

This index includes the names of the most significant places and physical features in Canada. Names are indexed to the Canadian regional maps in the Atlas of Canada section, and to the map of Canada on pages 44-45 in the World Atlas section. For an explanation of any abbreviations used in this index, refer to page 57 of the main index to the world atlas.

2F5 100 Mile House
3I5 Abbey
2F5 Abbotsford
3L1 Aberdeen Lake
7G1 Abitibi *r.*
7G1 Abitibi, Lake
7G4 Acton
7K3 Acton Vale
5K3 Adlavik Islands
6E2 Agawa *r.*
5J4 Aguanish *r.*
7G4 Ailsa Craig
2H5 Airdrie
7H4 Ajax
4E3 Akimiski Island
44E3 Aklavik
5I1 Akpatok Island
4E3 Albany *r.*
2H4 Alberta *prov.*
5K3 Alexis *r.*
2F4 Alexis Creek
7H3 Algonquin Park
5I5 Allardville
5H4 Alma
45K3 Amadjuak Lake
2D3 Ambition, Mount
5I5 Amherst
6F4 Amherstburg
7I3 Amherst Island
7H1 Amos
45I2 Amund Ringnes Island
44F2 Amundsen Gulf
6E1 Amyot
4F3 Anderson *r.*
3H4 Andrew
7H3 Angus
7G1 Ansonville
5J4 Anticosti, Île d' *i.*
5J5 Antigonish
3L5 Arborg
45J2 Arctic Bay
44C2 Arctic Ocean
44E3 Arctic Red *r.*
5I6 Argyle
7G4 Arkona
3J5 Arm *r.*
5H2 Arnaud *r.*
7I3 Arnprior
6C1 Arrow *r.*
7G4 Arthur
3I2 Artillery Lake
3M2 Arviat
6D1 Ashburton Bay
4D3 Asheweig *r.*
5I3 Ashuanipi *r.*
7K1 Ashuapmushuan *r.*
3J5 Assiniboia
3L5 Assiniboine *r.*
2H5 Assiniboine, Mount
3I3 Athabasca *r.*
3I3 Athabasca, Lake
7J3 Athens
4E3 Atikameg *r.*
4E3 Attawapiskat
4E3 Attawapiskat *r.*
6F2 Aubinadong *r.*
7G4 Auburn
4D4 Auden
7J2 Augustines, Lac des *l.*
5L5 Avalon Peninsula
45I2 Axel Heiberg Island
7G4 Aylmer
3I1 Aylmer Lake
2E4 Babine *r.*
3M1 Back *r.*
2D2 Backbone Ranges *mts*
45L2 Baffin Bay *sea*
45L3 Baffin Island
5H4 Baie-Comeau
5H5 Baie-St-Paul
3J1 Baillie *r.*
3M1 Baker Lake
3M1 Baker Lake *l.*
3K5 Baldy Mountain *hill*
7I3 Bancroft
2H5 Banff
2D4 Banks Island
44F2 Banks Island
3M2 Barbour Bay
7I1 Barraute
2H4 Barrhead
7H3 Barrie
5I6 Barrington
45I2 Barrow Strait
7I3 Barrys Bay
7J2 Baskatong, Réservoir
6E2 Batchawana *r.*
5I5 Bath
7I3 Bath
5I5 Bathurst
44F2 Bathurst, Cape
44H3 Bathurst Inlet (abandoned)
44H3 Bathurst Inlet *inlet*
45I2 Bathurst Island
3I4 Battle *r.*
3I4 Battleford
5L4 Bauld, Cape
7G4 Bayfield
7J2 Bazin *r.*
4E3 Bear Island
2F3 Beatton *r.*
7I1 Beattyville
44D2 Beaufort Sea
3H2 Beaulieu *r.*
3L5 Beauséjour
2E3 Beaver *r.*
3J4 Beaver *r.*
4D3 Beaver *r.*
2G4 Beaverlodge
5J5 Bedford
7K3 Bedford
4F2 Belcher Islands
7I1 Bell *r.*
2D4 Bella Bella
5L4 Belle Isle *i.*
5K4 Belle Isle, Strait of
7I3 Belleville
44F3 Belot, Lac *l.*
3L4 Berens *r.*
3L4 Berens River
2G4 Berland *r.*
5H4 Betsiamites *r.*
5K3 Big *r.*
3J4 Biggar
2C2 Big Salmon *r.*
3J4 Big Sandy Lake
3N4 Big Trout Lake
3H4 Big Valley
3H3 Birch *r.*
3M5 Birch Lake
7H3 Birch Mountains
2G3 Bistcho Lake
3L5 Black *r.*
6D1 Black *r.*
7G1 Black *r.*
3L5 Black Island
3J3 Black Lake
6C1 Black Sturgeon *r.*
7G4 Blenheim
3L5 Bloodvein *r.*
7I4 Bloomfield
2D3 Blue *r.*
2F3 Blueberry *r.*
7H3 Bobcaygeon
3K5 Boissevain
7H4 Bolton
5L4 Bonavista
3I4 Bonnyville
45J3 Boothia, Gulf of
45I2 Boothia Peninsula
45G2 Borden Island
45J2 Borden Peninsula
5H2 Borel *r.*
7G4 Bothwell
5L4 Botwood
7K3 Boucherville
7G1 Bourkes
3I5 Bow *r.*
7H3 Bracebridge
7H3 Bradford
7H4 Brampton
3L5 Brandon
7G4 Brantford
5J5 Bras d'Or Lake
2H4 Brazeau *r.*
5I5 Bridgetown
5I5 Bridgewater
7I3 Brighton
2F5 British Columbia *prov.*
4F4 Broadback *r.*
7J3 Brockville
45J2 Brodeur Peninsula
3L5 Brokenhead *r.*
3I5 Brooks
7G3 Bruce Peninsula
3J4 Bruno
5H1 Buet *r.*
2H2 Buffalo *r.*
2G3 Buffalo Head Hills
3I4 Buffalo Narrows
3K1 Bullen *r.*
5K5 Burgeo
5L5 Burin
5L5 Burin Peninsula
7H4 Burlington
2F5 Burnaby
44H3 Burnside *r.*
2E4 Burns Lake
3L4 Burntwood *r.*
5H2 Buron *r.*
45K2 Bylot Island
5H5 Cabano
7G3 Cabot Head
5J5 Cabot Strait
2G3 Cadotte *r.*
2G1 Calder *r.*
7H4 Caledonia
2H5 Calgary
7I2 Camachigama *r.*
7G4 Cambridge
45H3 Cambridge Bay
2G3 Cameron Hills
45H2 Cameron Island
7I3 Campbellford
3J2 Campbell Lake
2E5 Campbell River
7I3 Campbells Bay
5I5 Campbellton
3H4 Camrose
5I5 Canaan *r.*
5H3 Caniapiscau
5H2 Caniapiscau *r.*
5H3 Caniapiscau, Réservoir de *l.*
3K5 Canora
2E2 Canyon Ranges *mts*
5J5 Cap-aux-Meules
7K2 Cap-de-la-Madeleine
5J5 Cape Breton Island
5J5 Cape George
5I5 Caraquet
2D1 Carcajou *r.*
2H5 Cardston
2F4 Cariboo Mountains
2E2 Caribou *r.*
3M3 Caribou *r.*
45J4 Caribou Lake
2H3 Caribou Mountains
3K5 Carlyle
3L5 Carman
3K4 Carrot *r.*
7G2 Cartier
44F5 Cascade Range *mts*
2D2 Cassiar Mountains
2G5 Castlegar
4F3 Castor, Rivière du *r.*
5J2 Caubvick, Mount
5I4 Causapscal
7H4 Cayuga
3K4 Cedar Lake
5I4 Chaleur Bay *inlet*
5H3 Chambeaux, Lac *l.*
7K1 Chambord
7K3 Champlain, Lake
5I4 Chandler
5K5 Channel-Port-aux-Basques
6F2 Chapleau
3J5 Chaplin
5H5 Charlesbourg
3I3 Charles Lake
5J5 Charlottetown
3M4 Charron Lake
2G5 Chase
7K3 Châteauguay
5H2 Châteauguay *r.*
7F4 Chatham
7G3 Chatsworth
5I5 Chester
3N2 Chesterfield Inlet
3M2 Chesterfield Inlet *inlet*
7J3 Chesterville
2F4 Chetwynd
4G3 Chevreulx *r.*
4G4 Chibougamau
5H4 Chicoutimi
45L3 Chidley, Cape
2F4 Chilanko *r.*
2F5 Chilcotin *r.*
2F4 Chilko *r.*
2C3 Chilkoot Pass
2F5 Chilliwack
2G3 Chinchaga *r.*
5I5 Chipman
4F3 Chisasibi
45L2 Christian, Cape
3I3 Christina *r.*
3M3 Churchill
3M3 Churchill *r.*
5J3 Churchill *r.*
3M3 Churchill, Cape
3H3 Claire, Lake
5L4 Clarenville
2H5 Claresholm
2G3 Clear Hills
2H4 Clearwater *r.*
3I3 Clearwater *r.*
3J1 Clinton-Colden Lake
6C1 Cloud Bay
45L2 Clyde River
2E3 Coal *r.*
2E4 Coast Mountains
5H5 Coaticook
45J3 Coats Island
7I3 Cobden
3M4 Cobham *r.*
45K2 Coburg Island
2H5 Cochrane
7G1 Cochrane
3K3 Cochrane *r.*
5J2 Cod Island
7J4 Colborne
3I4 Cold Lake
2G5 Coldstream
3I5 Coleville
7G3 Collingwood
45H2 Collinson Peninsula
2G4 Columbia, Mount
2F4 Columbia Mountains
45J3 Committee Bay
4F3 Conn *r.*
3I4 Consort
7K3 Contrecoeur
3I1 Contwoyto Lake
7G2 Copper Cliff
2H1 Coppermine *r.*
2F5 Coquitlam
5K4 Corner Brook
7J3 Cornwall
45I2 Cornwallis Island
45I2 Cornwall Island
44G3 Coronation Gulf
7I3 Coulonge *r.*
2E5 Courtenay
6F2 Cow *r.*
7K3 Cowansville
2H5 Cranbrook
3J3 Cree *r.*
3J3 Cree Lake
7G3 Creemore
3K4 Creighton
2G5 Creston
7G3 Croker, Cape
3I4 Cross Lake
2H5 Crowsnest Pass
2H5 Crowsnest Pass *pass*
45L3 Cumberland Peninsula
45L3 Cumberland Sound *sea chan.*
3I5 Cypress Hills
3M4 Dafoe *r.*
5I4 Dalhousie
3J4 Dalmeny
5J5 Dartmouth
3K5 Dauphin
5J5 Davidson
5J3 Davis Inlet (abandoned)
45M3 Davis Strait
2B1 Dawson
2F4 Dawson Creek
2D3 Dease *r.*
44H3 Dease Strait
3J4 Debden
7I2 Deep River
3M4 Deer Lake
5H2 Delay *r.*
2F1 Déline
3K5 Deloraine
7I3 Denbigh
4F3 Denys *r.*
6F2 Devon
45I2 Devon Island
2H5 Didsbury
3I5 Diefenbaker, Lake
5I5 Digby
3I4 Dillon *r.*
5H5 Disraëli
2C4 Dixon Entrance *sea chan.*
6C1 Dog *r.*
6C1 Dog Lake
7K1 Dolbeau
2H4 Drayton Valley
7F4 Dresden
3H5 Drumheller
5G5 Drummondville
7K3 Drummondville
2C2 Drury Lake
3M5 Dryden
3L2 Dubawnt *r.*
3K2 Dubawnt Lake
4F2 Dufferin, Cape
7I2 Dumoine *r.*
2F5 Duncan
4F3 Duncan, Lac *l.*
7H4 Dundas
7H4 Dunnville
7G3 Durham
45L3 Dyer, Cape
5K3 Eagle *r.*
3J4 Eagle Creek *r.*
6C1 Eaglehead Lake
2G4 Eaglesham
4F3 Eastmain *r.*
5J5 East Point
7H4 East York
2G1 Echo Bay
6E2 Echo Bay
3M4 Echoing *r.*
2G4 Edith Cavell, Mount
2H4 Edmonton
5H5 Edmundston
2G4 Edson
2D3 Edziza, Mount
4E3 Ekwan *r.*
5J2 Eliot, Mount
2H5 Elk *r.*
2H5 Elkford
3I4 Elk Point
45H2 Ellef Ringnes Island
45J2 Ellesmere Island
3K1 Ellice *r.*
6F2 Elliot Lake
5J5 Elmira
7G4 Elmira
7J3 Embrun
2G2 Emile *r.*
2G5 Enderby
3M5 English *r.*
7G4 Erie, Lake
7G4 Erin
44E3 Eskimo Lakes
7G2 Espanola
2F5 Esquimalt
6F4 Essex
3K5 Estevan
7H4 Etobicoke
45J2 Eureka Sound *sea chan.*
2H4 Evansburg
3P2 Evans Strait
6F3 Evansville
7G4 Exeter
5L4 Exploits *r.*
2G3 Fairview
2B3 Fairweather, Mount
5H2 False *r.*
2G5 Farnham, Mount
3N4 Fawn *r.*
7G4 Fergus
5H2 Feuilles, Rivière aux *r.*
2E3 Finlay *r.*
2D2 Finlay, Mount
2F4 Finlay Forks
45J3 Fisher Strait
3M4 Flanagan *r.*
2E2 Flat *r.*
3K4 Flin Flon
6E1 Flint Lake
3K5 Foam Lake
3J3 Fond du Lac *r.*
2F3 Fontas *r.*
2G4 Forbes, Mount
2E4 Foresight Mountain
7G4 Forest
5H4 Forestville
4E3 Fort Albany
2H4 Fort Assiniboine
2F2 Fort Liard
2H5 Fort Macleod
3I3 Fort McMurray
2F3 Fort Nelson
2F3 Fort Nelson *r.*
2H4 Fort Saskatchewan
4D2 Fort Severn
2F2 Fort Simpson
3H2 Fort Smith
2E4 Fort St James
2F3 Fort St John
5L5 Fortune Bay
2E3 Fox *r.*
3M3 Fox *r.*
2G4 Fox Creek
45K3 Foxe Basin *g.*
45K3 Foxe Channel
45K3 Foxe Peninsula
7I3 Frankford
2F2 Franklin Mountains
45I2 Franklin Strait
2F5 Fraser *r.*
5J2 Fraser *r.*
7G1 Fraserdale
2E4 Fraser Lake
2E4 Fraser Plateau
7G1 Frederick House *r.*
5I5 Fredericton
45L3 Frobisher Bay
3N2 Fullerton, Cape
5I5 Fundy, Bay of *g.*
5K4 Gambo
7I3 Gananoque
5L4 Gander
7G1 Gardiner
6E2 Gargantua, Cape
2F5 Garibaldi, Mount
5I4 Gaspé
5I4 Gaspé, Cap *c.*
5I4 Gaspé, Péninsule de la *pen.*
2E3 Gataga *r.*
7J3 Gatineau
7J3 Gatineau *r.*
3L3 Gauer Lake
3K3 Geikie *r.*
5I2 George *r.*
7G3 Georgian Bay
6D1 Geraldton
45J2 Gifford *r.*
3M3 Gillam
4G3 Gipouloux *r.*
5K5 Glace Bay
3L5 Glenboro
7G4 Glencoe
6E2 Glendale
5L4 Glovertown
7G4 Goderich
3M3 Gods *r.*
3O1 Gordon *r.*
7J1 Gouin, Réservoir
6B1 Graham
2C4 Graham Island
45I2 Graham Island
7K3 Granby
5L5 Grand Bank
5I5 Grand Bay
7G4 Grand Bend
2G4 Grande Cache
2G4 Grande Prairie
5I5 Grand Falls
5L4 Grand Falls
2G5 Grand Forks
5G5 Grand-Mère
7K2 Grand-Mère
3L4 Grand Rapids
3L3 Grass *r.*
7H3 Gravenhurst
2E3 Grayling *r.*
2E1 Great Bear *r.*
2G1 Great Bear Lake
3I5 Great Sand Hills
2H2 Great Slave Lake
2E3 Great Snow Mountain
3K5 Grenfell
5L4 Grey Islands
2G3 Grimshaw
7G1 Groundhog *r.*
5H2 Guè, Rivière du *r.*
7G4 Guelph
3L4 Gunisao *r.*
2F3 Halfway *r.*
7H3 Haliburton
7H3 Haliburton Highlands *hills*
5J5 Halifax
45L3 Hall Peninsula
7H3 Halls Lake
7H4 Hamilton
5K3 Hamilton Inlet
3I5 Hanna
7G3 Hanover
5J3 Happy Valley - Goose Bay
2H3 Harper Creek *r.*
7H1 Harricana, Rivière d' *r.*
5K3 Harrison, Cape
44E3 Hart *r.*
7I3 Hastings
3J4 Haultain *r.*
7I3 Havelock
5J4 Havre-St-Pierre
5K4 Hawkes Bay
7J3 Hawkesbury
2H2 Hay *r.*
3M3 Hayes *r.*
45I3 Hayes *r.*
44G3 Hay River
45G2 Hazen Strait
6F1 Hearst
5J2 Hebron
2D4 Hecate Strait
7K3 Hemmingford
4E3 Henrietta Maria, Cape
7G4 Hensall
2C2 Hess *r.*
2C2 Hess Mountains
2G3 High Level
2G4 High Prairie
2H5 High River
2G4 Hinton
45L3 Home Bay
5I4 Honguedo, Détroit d' *sea chan.*
2F5 Hope
4F2 Hopewell Islands
2G2 Horn *r.*
6E1 Hornepayne
2F2 Horn Mountains
2D2 Horn Peak
5L4 Horse Islands
44F3 Horton *r.*
2G1 Hottah Lake
2E4 Houston
7K3 Howick
5I2 Hubbard, Pointe *pt*
3K4 Hudson Bay
45J4 Hudson Bay *sea*
45K3 Hudson Strait
3K3 Hughes *r.*
7J3 Hull
3J4 Humboldt
2D1 Hume *r.*
7J3 Huntingdon
7H3 Huntsville
7G3 Hurd, Cape
6F3 Huron, Lake
5G3 Iberville, Lac d' *l.*
6B1 Ignace
2B2 Indian *r.*
3K5 Indian Head
2E3 Ingenika *r.*
7G4 Ingersoll
2C3 Inklin *r.*
2H4 Innisfail
4F2 Inukjuak
44E3 Inuvik
5J5 Inverness
45L3 Iqaluit
6F2 Iron Bridge
7G1 Iroquois Falls
2F2 Island *r.*
3M4 Island Lake
45K3 Ivujivik
5I4 Jacques-Cartier, Détroit de *sea chan.*
5I4 Jacques-Cartier, Mont *mt*
4E3 James Bay
45I3 James Ross Strait
2G4 Jasper
6D1 Jellicoe
2C3 Jennings *r.*
7K2 Joliette
45J2 Jones Sound *sea chan.*
5H4 Jonquière
44F5 Juan de Fuca Strait
6E1 Kabinakagami *r.*
6E1 Kabinakagami Lake
2G4 Kakwa *r.*
7I3 Kaladar
2E4 Kalone Peak
2F5 Kamloops
3K5 Kamsack
4F3 Kanaaupscow *r.*
5K3 Kanairiktok *r.*
5I2 Kangiqsualujjuaq
5H1 Kangirsuk
4E3 Kapiskau *r.*
6F1 Kapuskasing
3K2 Kasba Lake
3K3 Kasmere Lake
3M2 Kazan *r.*
2E3 Kechika *r.*
5I5 Kedgwick
2E1 Keele *r.*
2D2 Keele Peak
3M5 Keewatin
2F1 Keith Arm *b.*
2G5 Kelowna
3K4 Kelvington
7H2 Kenabeek
45J3 Kendall, Cape
4D4 Kenogami *r.*
3M5 Kenora
44H3 Kent Peninsula
3I5 Kerrobert
7H3 Keswick
2G5 Kettle *r.*
7G3 Key Harbour
2G5 Kicking Horse Pass
7G3 Killarney
2G4 Kinbasket Lake
3J5 Kincaid
7G3 Kincardine
3I5 Kindersley
4F2 King George Islands
2E4 King Island
7I3 Kingston
45I3 King William Island
4E3 Kinushseo *r.*
7H3 Kirkfield
7G1 Kirkland Lake
7G4 Kitchener
2D4 Kitimat
2C4 Knox, Cape
2G5 Kootenay *r.*
2G5 Kootenay Lake
44G3 Kugluktuk
5H2 Kuujjuaq
4F3 Kuujjuarapik
5H4 La Baie
5I2 La Baleine, Rivière à *r.*
7J2 Labelle
5J3 Labrador *reg.*
5I3 Labrador City
45M3 Labrador Sea
7K2 Lac-aux-Sables
7K1 Lac Bouchette
3L5 Lac du Bonnet
3I4 Lac La Biche
2H4 Lacombe
2G2 Laferte *r.*
5G3 Laforge *r.*
4G3 La Grande 3, Réservoir
5G3 La Grande 4, Réservoir
45K4 La Grande 4, Réservoir
7H3 Lakefield
5J5 La Madeleine, Îles de *is*
5H5 La Malbaie
2G2 La Martre, Lac *l.*
7G4 Lambeth
7J3 Lanark
7J3 Lancaster
45J2 Lancaster Sound *strait*
3K5 Langenburg
2F5 Langley
3J5 Lanigan
5G2 La Potherie, Lac *l.*
7G2 Larchwood
7G1 Larder Lake
3J4 La Ronge
3J4 La Ronge, Lac *l.*
7K3 LaSalle
7H1 La Sarre
5L4 La Scie
7K2 La Tuque
7K3 Laval
2D4 Laxgalts'ap
2D4 Lax Kw'alaams
6F4 Leamington
4G2 L'Eau Claire, Lac à *l.*
7I1 Lebel-sur-Quévillon
2H4 Leduc
5H2 Lefroy *r.*
4D4 Legarde *r.*
45L3 Lemieux Islands
5H1 Lepellé *r.*
5I5 Lepreau, Point
2H4 Lesser Slave Lake
3H5 Lethbridge
5H5 Lévis
2E2 Liard Plateau
7J3 Limoges
7H3 Lindsay
7K2 Linton
2F5 Lions Bay
7G4 Listowel
3M3 Little Churchill *r.*
7G3 Little Current
4D4 Little Current *r.*
5I5 Liverpool
3I4 Lloydminster
6E1 Lochalsh
2E2 Logan, Mount
2F5 Logan Lake
2D2 Logan Mountains
7G4 London
6D1 Longlac
7G4 Long Point *pt*
7G4 Long Point *pt*
7G4 Long Point Bay
5K4 Long Range Mountains
5K5 Long Range Mountains
7K3 Longueuil
2H3 Loon *r.*
4F3 Louis-XIV, Pointe *pt*
45L3 Low, Cape
2G5 Lower Arrow Lake
7G4 Lucknow
3J5 Lumsden
3M1 Lunan Lake
7G4 Luther Lake
3I2 Lutsel'k'e
2D4 Lyell Island
3J2 Lynx Lake
3I3 MacKay *r.*
3I2 MacKay Lake
2F4 Mackenzie
2F2 Mackenzie *r.*
44E3 Mackenzie Bay
45G2 Mackenzie King Island
2C1 Mackenzie Mountains
2C2 Macmillan *r.*
7I3 Madawaska *r.*
7I3 Madoc
3K4 Mafeking
5G5 Magog
5I4 Maggie *r.*
6E2 Magpie *r.*
4F4 Maicasagi *r.*
45L5 Maine, Gulf of
5H4 Manicouagan
5H4 Manicouagan *r.*
5H4 Manicouagan, Réservoir
3L4 Manitoba *prov.*
3L5 Manitoba, Lake
7F3 Manitoulin Island
7J2 Maniwaki
2G3 Manning
5H4 Manouane *r.*
45K3 Mansel Island
3I5 Maple Creek
3I1 Mara *r.*
6D1 Marathon
4F2 Marcopeet Islands
4F2 Mariet *r.*
7G3 Markdale
7H4 Markham
2F2 Martin *r.*
5L3 Mary's Harbour
7K3 Mascouche
7F2 Massey
4F4 Matagami
4F4 Matagami, Lac *l.*
5I4 Matane
7K2 Matawin *r.*
7G1 Mattagami *r.*
7H2 Mattawa
7I3 Maynooth
5I5 McAdam
45H2 McClintock Channel
44G2 McClure Strait
2F4 McCrea *r.*
2F4 McGregor *r.*
7G2 McGregor Bay
2G4 McLennan
2H4 McLeod *r.*
2F4 McLeod Lake
2B2 McQuesten *r.*
2G1 McTavish Arm *b.*
2F1 McVicar Arm *b.*
3I4 Meadow Lake
7G3 Meaford
5K3 Mealy Mountains
3I5 Medicine Hat
2G3 Meikle *r.*
2E2 Meilleur *r.*
2D2 Meister *r.*
6F3 Meldrum Bay
3J4 Melfort
3K5 Melita
3K5 Melville
45H2 Melville Island
45J3 Melville Peninsula
45L3 Mercy, Cape
2F5 Merritt
7I2 Messines
5H4 Métabetchouan
6E2 Michipicoten Bay
7K1 Micosas *r.*
5I5 Middleton
7H3 Midland
2H3 Mikkwa *r.*
7K2 Milieu *r.*
7H3 Millbrook
6B1 Mille Lacs, Lac des *l.*
2H4 Millet
3L5 Minnedosa
44G2 Minto Inlet
5I5 Miramichi
4E4 Missinaibi *r.*
4D3 Missisa *r.*
4F4 Missisicabi *r.*
6F2 Mississagi *r.*
7H4 Mississauga
7I3 Mississippi *r.*
5J4 Mistanipisipou *r.*
45K5 Mistassibi *r.*
7K1 Mistassini
5G4 Mistassini *r.*
4G4 Mistassini, Lac *l.*
7G4 Mitchell
5I4 Moisie *r.*
2G5 Monashee Mountains
5I5 Moncton
7J3 Montebello
5H4 Mont-Joli
7J2 Mont-Laurier
5H5 Montmagny
7K3 Montréal
6E2 Montreal *r.*
7H2 Montreal *r.*
3J4 Montreal Lake
6E2 Montreal River
4E4 Moose *r.*
3J5 Moose Jaw
3J5 Moose Jaw *r.*
3K5 Moose Mountain Creek *r.*
4E4 Moosonee
3L5 Morden
2C4 Moresby Island
7G4 Morpeth
3L5 Morris
3K4 Mossy *r.*
3I4 Mostoos Hills
2D1 Mountain *r.*
7G4 Mount Forest
5L5 Mount Pearl
5I2 Mucalic *r.*
3J3 Mudjatik *r.*
4D3 Muketei *r.*
3L4 Mukutawa *r.*
5L4 Musgrave Harbour
7G2 Muskeg *r.*
2C2 Nadaleen *r.*
6E1 Nagagami *r.*
2F2 Nahanni Range *mts*
2C3 Nakina *r.*
2G5 Nakusp
2F5 Nanaimo
45I1 Nansen Sound *sea chan.*
7G4 Nanticoke
3H1 Napaktulik Lake
7K3 Napierville
45K2 Nares Strait
5I3 Naskaupi *r.*
2D4 Nass *r.*
4F2 Nastapoca *r.*
4F2 Nastapoka Islands
5J4 Natashquan *r.*
2D2 Natla *r.*
3L5 Neepawa
2G5 Nelson
3M3 Nelson *r.*
2F3 Nelson Forks
4F4 Némiscau *r.*
7I3 Nepean
5I5 Nepisiguit *r.*
45K3 Nettilling Lake
7I3 Newboro
5I5 New Brunswick *prov.*
5I4 New Carlisle
7H4 Newcastle
5K4 Newfoundland *i.*
5K3 Newfoundland and Labrador *prov.*
5J5 New Glasgow
7H2 New Liskeard
7H3 Newmarket
7H4 Niagara Falls
7H4 Niagara-on-the-Lake
6F2 Nicholson
7K2 Nicolet
7G1 Nighthawk Lake
3J4 Nipawin
6C1 Nipigon
6C1 Nipigon *r.*
6C1 Nipigon, Lake
7H2 Nipissing, Lake
3N3 Niskibi *r.*
2B2 Nisling *r.*
2C2 Nisutlin *r.*
7I3 Noire *r.*
3I2 Nonacho Lake
7H1 Noranda
7K1 Normandin
3I4 North Battleford
7H2 North Bay
5I5 North Cape
6F2 North Channel *lake channel*
4E4 North French *r.*
3M3 North Knife *r.*
3J4 North Saskatchewan *r.*
3L3 North Seal *r.*
5I5 Northumberland Strait
2F5 North Vancouver
44F3 Northwest Territories *admin. div.*
7H4 North York
7I3 Norway Bay
7G4 Norwich
5J2 Notakwanon *r.*
2G3 Notikewin *r.*
5H5 Notre-Dame, Monts *mts*
5L4 Notre Dame Bay
7J3 Notre-Dame-de-la-Salette
7H2 Notre-Dame-du-Nord
7G3 Nottawasaga Bay
4F4 Nottaway *r.*
3J5 Notukeu Creek *r.*
5I6 Nova Scotia *prov.*
3L2 Nueltin Lake
4G1 Nunavik *reg.*
45I3 Nunavut *admin. div.*
2H2 Nyarling *r.*
7H4 Oakville
3L3 Odei *r.*
6E2 Ogidaki
44E3 Ogilvie *r.*
44D3 Ogilvie Mountains
4D4 Ogoki *r.*
2G5 Okanagan Lake
2I5 Oldman *r.*
2H5 Olds
4F4 Olga, Lac *l.*
5J4 Olomane *r.*
4D4 Ontario *prov.*
7I4 Ontario, Lake
6F1 Opasatika *r.*
4F3 Opinaca *r.*
4E3 Opinnagau *r.*
5H3 Opiscotéo, Lac *l.*
7G4 Orangeville
6C1 Orient Bay
7H3 Orillia
7K3 Ormstown
5I5 Oromocto
6E1 Osawin *r.*
7J3 Osgoode
7H4 Oshawa
2E3 Osilinka *r.*
2G5 Osoyoos
5I3 Ossokmanuan Lake
3N5 Otoskwin *r.*
7J3 Ottawa
4E2 Ottawa Islands
7J3 Outaouais, Rivière des *r.*
5H4 Outardes, Rivière aux *r.*
3J5 Outlook
7G3 Owen Sound
3M3 Owl *r.*
3K5 Oxbow
3I5 Oyen
6E1 Pagwachuan *r.*
7G4 Palmerston
45L3 Pangnirtung
7J3 Papineauville
7I1 Paradis
5K3 Paradise *r.*
3I4 Paradise Hill
7J2 Parent
7G4 Paris
6F2 Parkinson
45G2 Parry Channel
45G2 Parry Islands
7G3 Parry Sound
4E4 Partridge *r.*
7J1 Pascagama *r.*
3K4 Pasquia Hills
2I3 Peace *r.*
2G3 Peace River
45I2 Peary Channel
44E2 Peel *r.*
6F5 Pelee Island
7F5 Pelee Point
2C2 Pelly *r.*
2C2 Pelly Mountains
6F2 Pemache *r.*
2F5 Pemberton
2H4 Pembina *r.*
7J2 Pembroke
7H3 Penetanguishene
2G5 Penticton
5I4 Percé
7I3 Perth
5I5 Perth-Andover
7H3 Petawawa
7H3 Peterborough
5K4 Petit Mécatina *r.*
2F2 Petitot *r.*
7I4 Petre, Point
7F4 Petrolia
4F3 Piagochioui *r.*
6D1 Pic *r.*
7H4 Pickering
7I4 Picton
5J5 Pictou
7G3 Pike Bay
2H5 Pincher Creek
3L5 Pine Falls
3N4 Pineimuta *r.*
3N4 Pipestone *r.*
5H4 Pipmuacan, Réservoir
5I3 Pitaga
2D4 Pitt Island
4E4 Pivabiska *r.*
5L5 Placentia
5L5 Placentia Bay
5L5 Plaster Rock
7G2 Pogamasing
7K1 Pointe-Bleue
2H1 Point Lake
2H4 Ponoka
5H2 Pons *r.*
4F4 Pontax *r.*
3L4 Poplar *r.*
5K3 Porcupine, Cape
3K4 Porcupine Hills
3L5 Portage la Prairie
2E5 Port Alberni
2E5 Port Alice
5K4 Port aux Choix
7H3 Port Bolster
5I4 Port-Cartier
7G3 Port Elgin
7H4 Port Hope
2E5 Port McNeill
5H4 Portneuf *r.*
7H3 Port Perry
7H3 Port Severn
5L5 Pouch Cove
2E5 Powell River
3K4 Prairie River
3K5 Preeceville
3J4 Prince Albert
44G2 Prince Albert Peninsula
44F2 Prince Alfred, Cape
45K3 Prince Charles Island
5J5 Prince Edward Island *prov.*
2F4 Prince George
45I2 Prince of Wales Island
44G2 Prince of Wales Strait
44G2 Prince Patrick Island
45I2 Prince Regent Inlet *sea chan.*
2D4 Prince Rupert
2D4 Princess Royal Island
2F5 Princeton
6E3 Prophet *r.*
6E1 Pukaskwa *r.*
2G5 Purcell Mountains
4F1 Puvurnituq
45L3 Qikiqtarjuaq
3K5 Qu'Appelle *r.*
45L3 Quaqtaq
5H5 Québec
45K4 Québec *prov.*
2C4 Queen Charlotte
2C4 Queen Charlotte Islands
2D5 Queen Charlotte Sound *sea chan.*
2E5 Queen Charlotte Strait
45H2 Queen Elizabeth Islands
45H3 Queen Maud Gulf
2F4 Quesnel
3M1 Quoich *r.*
7I3 Quyon
2E3 Rabbit *r.*
2F2 Rabbitskin *r.*
5L5 Race, Cape
2G2 Rae-Edzo
5H4 Ragueneau
2G3 Rainbow Lake
6C1 Raith
2F2 Ram *r.*
6F2 Ramsey
2D2 Rancheria
2D2 Rancheria *r.*
7H2 Rapide-Deux
7K2 Rawdon
5K5 Ray, Cape
2E3 Red *r.*
5K4 Red Bay
2H4 Red Deer
3I5 Red Deer *r.*
3K4 Red Deer *r.*
2G2 Redknife *r.*
3M5 Red Lake
2E5 Redonda Island
6C1 Red Rock
2E1 Redstone *r.*
7G1 Redstone *r.*
2H4 Redwater
3J5 Regina
3K4 Reindeer *r.*
3L4 Reindeer Island
3K3 Reindeer Lake
3I2 Reliance
7I3 Renfrew
45J3 Repulse Bay
45L3 Resolution Island
5I5 Restigouche *r.*
2G5 Revelstoke
44E3 Richards Island
3I3 Richardson *r.*
44E3 Richardson Mountains
7J3 Richmond
7J3 Rideau *r.*
7I3 Rideau Lakes
4D4 Ridge *r.*
7G4 Ridgetown
7J3 Rigaud
2H4 Rimbey
5H4 Rimouski
3J5 Riverhurst
5I5 Riverview
7K2 Rivière-à-Pierre
7K2 Rivière-aux-Rats
5H5 Rivière-du-Loup
4F3 Robert-Bourassa, Réservoir
7K1 Roberval
2C2 Robinson Mountains
3K5 Roblin
2G4 Robson, Mount
2E2 Rock *r.*
7J3 Rockland
5K4 Rocky Harbour
2H4 Rocky Mountain House
44H5 Rocky Mountains
45J3 Roes Welcome Sound *sea chan.*
4F3 Roggan *r.*
5J4 Romaine *r.*
2E3 Roosevelt, Mount
2F2 Root *r.*
2H5 Rosebud *r.*
2D4 Rose Point
3J5 Rosetown
2G5 Rossland
7H1 Rouyn
4F4 Rupert *r.*
3K5 Russell
7J3 Russell
7H2 Rutherglen
2F5 Saanich
5I6 Sable, Cape
5K6 Sable Island
7F2 Sables, River aux *r.*
45H2 Sachs Harbour
5I5 Sackville
5H4 Saguenay *r.*
2H4 St Albert
7K2 St-Alexis-des-Monts
7J3 St-André-Avellin
5L4 St Anthony
5K4 St-Augustin
5K4 St Augustin *r.*
7H4 St Catharines
7K3 St-Césaire
6F4 St Clair, Lake
7J3 Ste-Adèle
7J2 Ste-Agathe-des-Monts
3L5 Sainte Anne
7J2 Ste-Anne-du-Lac
7K2 Ste-Émélie-de-l'Énergie
7K3 Ste-Julienne
2A2 St Elias Mountains
5I4 Ste-Marguerite *r.*
3L5 Sainte Rose du Lac
7K3 Ste-Thérèse
7K3 St-Eustache
7J2 Ste-Véronique
5H4 St-Fabien
7K1 St-Félicien
7K2 St-Félix-de-Valois
7K2 St-François *r.*
7K2 St-Gabriel
5H5 St-Georges
5K4 St George's Bay
7K3 St-Hyacinthe
7K2 St-Ignace-du-Lac
7H1 St-Jacques-de-Dupuy
5I4 St-Jean *r.*
7K1 St-Jean, Lac *l.*
7K3 St-Jean-sur-Richelieu
4G5 St-Jérôme
7J3 St-Jérôme
5I5 Saint John
5L5 St John's
3N5 St Joseph, Lake
7J2 St-Jovité
5L5 St Lawrence
7K3 St Lawrence *inlet*
5J4 St Lawrence, Gulf of
7J3 St Lawrence Seaway *sea chan.*
7K2 St-Léonard
5K3 St Lewis *r.*
7K2 St-Louis-de-France
7G4 St Mary's
7H1 St-Mathieu
7K2 St-Maurice *r.*
7K2 St-Michel-des-Saints
5H5 St-Pacôme
5H5 St Pascal
5K4 St Paul *r.*
7K3 St-Pie
7K3 St-Rémi
7J3 St-Sauveur-des-Monts
5H5 St Siméon
7G4 St Thomas
7G4 St Williams
4F3 Sakami *r.*
4F3 Sakami Lake
7J3 Salaberry-de-Valleyfield
2G5 Salmon Arm
6E2 Sand Lake
3M4 Sandy Lake
4F2 Sanikiluaq
7F4 Sarnia
3J4 Saskatchewan *prov.*
3K4 Saskatchewan *r.*
3J4 Saskatoon
2H2 Sass *r.*
6E2 Sault Sainte Marie
5H4 Savane *r.*
7H4 Scarborough
5I3 Schefferville
6D1 Schreiber
2D5 Scott, Cape
7G4 Seaforth
3M3 Seal *r.*
2F5 Sechelt
6B1 Seine *r.*
3L5 Selkirk
2G4 Selkirk Mountains
2C2 Selous, Mount
3J2 Selwyn Lake
2D1 Selwyn Mountains
7I1 Senneterre
7K2 Sentinel Peak
5I4 Sept-Îles
5H3 Sérigny *r.*
3M5 Seul, Lac *l.*
4D3 Severn *r.*
4D3 Shagamu *r.*
7K2 Shawinigan
5I5 Shediac
6E1 Shekak *r.*
5I6 Shelburne
7G3 Shelburne
3J4 Shellbrook
5H5 Sherbrooke
2C3 Sheslay *r.*
2G5 Sicamous
6C1 Silver Islet
7G4 Simcoe
7H3 Simcoe, Lake
2G4 Simonette *r.*
7G3 Singhampton
3N5 Sioux Lookout
2E2 Sir James MacBrien, Mount
2G5 Sir Sandford, Mount
2G4 Sir Wilfrid Laurier, Mount
2D4 Skeena *r.*
2D3 Skeena Mountains
3H2 Slave *r.*
2H4 Slave Lake
2H2 Slave Point
4F2 Sleeper Islands
5I3 Smallwood Reservoir
7I3 Smiths Falls
7G1 Smooth Rock Falls
2C1 Snake *r.*
2G2 Snare *r.*
3I2 Snowdrift *r.*
3K4 Snow Lake
5L3 Snug Harbour
45I2 Somerset Island
7K2 Sorel
3K5 Souris
3L5 Souris *r.*
7G3 Southampton
45J3 Southampton Island
7F3 South Baymouth
3L3 Southern Indian Lake
7H3 South River
3J4 South Saskatchewan *r.*
3L3 South Seal *r.*
6F2 Spanish
7F2 Spanish *r.*
2G4 Spirit River
7F3 Spring Bay
5L4 Springdale
5I5 Springhill
2H4 Spruce Grove
7G3 Stayner
6D1 Steel *r.*
2G3 Steen *r.*
45H2 Stefansson Island
3L5 Steinbach
3H4 Stettler
2B2 Stewart *r.*
2C3 Stikine *r.*
2D3 Stikine Plateau
7I3 Stirling
3L5 Stonewall
4E3 Stooping *r.*
7G4 Stratford
2H5 Strathmore
7G4 Strathroy
3M4 Stupart *r.*
3J4 Sturgeon *r.*
7H2 Sturgeon *r.*
7H2 Sturgeon Falls
7G2 Sudbury
6F2 Sultan
5L4 Summerford
2H5 Sundre
7H3 Sundridge
6D2 Superior, Lake
2F5 Surrey
7K3 Sutton
4E3 Sutton *r.*
45I2 Sverdrup Islands
5H2 Swampy *r.*
3K4 Swan *r.*
4E3 Swan *r.*
2H4 Swan Hills
3K4 Swan River
3J5 Swift Current
3J5 Swiftcurrent Creek *r.*
5J5 Sydney
5J5 Sydney Mines
2H4 Sylvan Lake
3H5 Taber
3L3 Tadoule Lake
2C2 Tagish
2E4 Tahtsa Peak
2C3 Taku
3H2 Taltson *r.*
3K1 Tammarvi *r.*
2D3 Tanzilla *r.*
5H2 Tasiujaq
2E4 Tatuk Mountain
2C2 Tay *r.*
2F3 Taylor
3I2 Tazin *r.*
7G3 Teeswater
7H2 Temagami Lake
5G4 Témiscamie *r.*
6F2 Tenby Bay
2D4 Terrace
6D1 Terrace Bay
2C2 Teslin *r.*
3M2 Tha-anne *r.*
7F4 Thames *r.*
3L1 Thelon *r.*
3K4 The Pas
6F2 Thessalon
5H5 Thetford Mines
3M2 Thlewiaza *r.*
3I2 Thoa *r.*
3L4 Thompson
2F5 Thompson *r.*
2E5 Thompson Sound
7I3 Thousand Islands
2H5 Three Hills
6C1 Thunder Bay
6C1 Thunder Bay *b.*
3J5 Thunder Creek *r.*
5G4 Tichégami *r.*
6F4 Tilbury
7G4 Tillsonburg
7G1 Timmins
7I1 Tionaga
2E3 Toad *r.*
7G3 Tobermory
3K4 Tobin Lake
2E5 Tofino
7H2 Tomiko
3K4 Tonto *r.*
2H5 Tornado Mountain
5I2 Torngat Mountains
7H4 Toronto
7K2 Tracy
4C4 Trading *r.*
2G5 Trail
7J2 Tremblant, Mont *hill*
2E4 Trembleur Lake
7K2 Trenche *r.*
5L5 Trepassey
5L5 Trinity Bay
7K2 Trois-Rivières
2E3 Trout *r.*
2G2 Trout *r.*
7H3 Trout Creek
2F2 Trout Lake
2F2 Trout Lake *l.*
3M5 Trout Lake *l.*
5J5 Truro
2F4 Tumbler Ridge
2D2 Tungsten (abandoned)
7G1 Tunis
5I2 Tunulic *r.*
7H1 Turgeon *r.*
2E3 Turnagain *r.*
2H5 Turner Valley
7I3 Tweed
5I3 Twin Falls
4F2 Umiujaq
4G1 Ungava, Péninsule d' *pen.*
3I2 Ungava Bay
3I4 Unity
2G5 Upper Arrow Lake
3I3 Uranium City
7H3 Uxbridge
7I1 Val-d'Or
5H5 Vallée-Jonction
2F5 Vancouver
2E5 Vancouver Island
2E4 Vanderhoof
4F3 Vauquelin *r.*
3H5 Vauxhall
3H4 Vegreville
3I4 Vermilion
7K2 Vermillon *r.*
7G2 Verner
2G5 Vernon
5H4 Vert, Île *i.*
2F5 Victoria
44H2 Victoria Island
5H5 Victoriaville
7H2 Ville-Marie
3K5 Virden
45G2 Viscount Melville Sound *sea chan.*
4C4 Wabakimi Lake
7H3 Wabasca *r.*
4D4 Wabassi *r.*
5I3 Wabush
2E5 Waddington, Mount
3K5 Wadena
3I4 Wainwright
3J4 Wakaw
7J3 Wakefield
3L4 Walker Lake
7G3 Walkerton
7F4 Wallaceburg
3I2 Walmsley Lake
2G4 Wapiti *r.*
3J4 Warman
7G3 Wasaga Beach
4F4 Waskaganish
4F4 Waswanipi *r.*
7G4 Waterloo
7K3 Waterloo
7G4 Watford
3K3 Wathaman *r.*
3J5 Watrous
3J4 Watson
2D2 Watson Lake
6E2 Wawa
7H1 Wawagosic *r.*
4D3 Webequie
7J3 Weir
7H4 Welland
7G4 Wellesley
7I4 Wellington
5K3 West Bay
2H4 Westlock
7G4 West Lorne
2H4 Wetaskiwin
3K5 Weyburn
7H4 Whitby
7H4 Whitchurch-Stouffville
6D1 White *r.*
5K4 White Bay
2H4 Whitecourt
2E1 Whitefish *r.*
3J2 Whitefish Lake
2C2 Whitehorse
2G3 Whitemud *r.*
2C3 White Pass
2H2 Whitesand *r.*
3K5 Whitewood
3J2 Wholdaia Lake
7G3 Wiarton
6C1 Wild Goose
3I4 Wilkie
2D3 Will, Mount
2F4 Williams Lake
2F4 Williston Lake
2F2 Willowlake *r.*
7J3 Winchester
2C1 Wind *r.*
7K2 Windigo *r.*
5I5 Windsor
6F4 Windsor
7G4 Wingham
4D3 Winisk *r.*
3L5 Winnipeg
3L5 Winnipeg *r.*
3L5 Winnipeg, Lake
3K4 Winnipegosis, Lake
2C2 Wolf *r.*
5I5 Wolfville
3K3 Wollaston Lake
44G3 Wollaston Peninsula
3L5 Woodridge
45I5 Woods, Lake of the
5I5 Woodstock
7G4 Woodstock
7H3 Woodville
3J5 Wynyard
2F5 Yale
5I6 Yarmouth
2H2 Yates *r.*
2H2 Yellowknife
2H2 Yellowknife *r.*
7H4 York
3K5 Yorkton
2B2 Yukon *r.*
2C2 Yukon Territory *admin. div.*

Collins
World Atlas

Collins

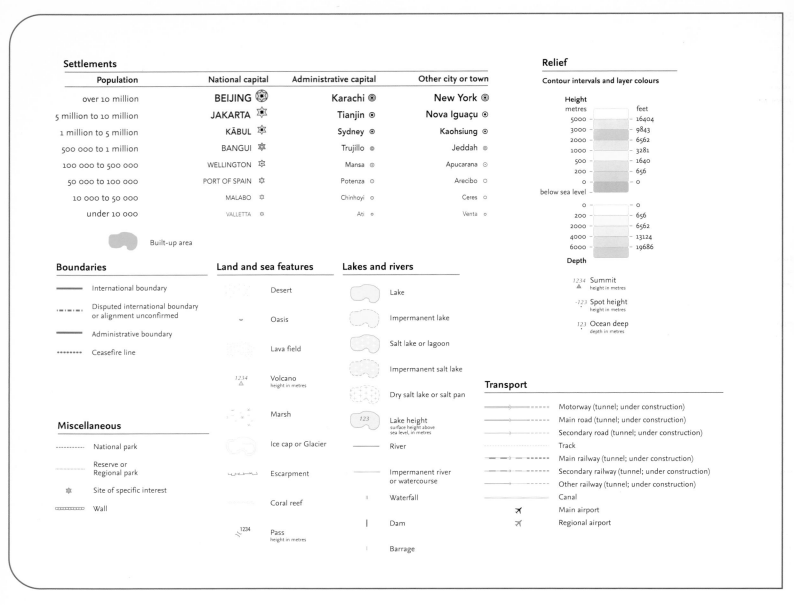

Settlements

Population	National capital	Administrative capital	Other city or town
over 10 million	**BEIJING**	**Karachi**	**New York**
5 million to 10 million	**JAKARTA**	**Tianjin**	**Nova Iguaçu**
1 million to 5 million	**KĀBUL**	**Sydney**	**Kaohsiung**
500 000 to 1 million	BANGUI	Trujillo	Jeddah
100 000 to 500 000	WELLINGTON	Mansa	Apucarana
50 000 to 100 000	PORT OF SPAIN	Potenza	Arecibo
10 000 to 50 000	MALABO	Chinhoyi	Ceres
under 10 000	VALLETTA	Ati	Venta

Built-up area

Boundaries

International boundary

Disputed international boundary or alignment unconfirmed

Administrative boundary

Ceasefire line

Miscellaneous

National park

Reserve or Regional park

Site of specific interest

Wall

Land and sea features

Desert

Oasis

Lava field

1234 Volcano
height in metres

Marsh

Ice cap or Glacier

Escarpment

Coral reef

1234 Pass
height in metres

Lakes and rivers

Lake

Impermanent lake

Salt lake or lagoon

Impermanent salt lake

Dry salt lake or salt pan

123 Lake height
surface height above
sea level, in metres

River

Impermanent river or watercourse

Waterfall

Dam

Barrage

Relief

Contour intervals and layer colours

Height

metres	feet
5000	16404
3000	9843
2000	6562
1000	3281
500	1640
200	656
0	0
below sea level	
200	656
2000	6562
4000	13124
6000	19686

Depth

1234 ▲ Summit
height in metres

-123 Spot height
height in metres

123 Ocean deep
depth in metres

Transport

Motorway (tunnel; under construction)

Main road (tunnel; under construction)

Secondary road (tunnel; under construction)

Track

Main railway (tunnel; under construction)

Secondary railway (tunnel; under construction)

Other railway (tunnel; under construction)

Canal

Main airport

Regional airport

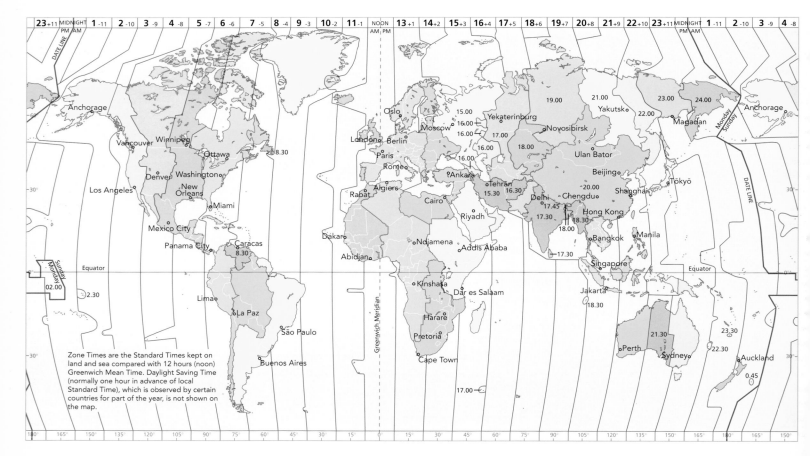

Zone Times are the Standard Times kept on land and sea compared with 12 hours (noon) Greenwich Mean Time. Daylight Saving Time (normally one hour in advance of local Standard Time), which is observed by certain countries for part of the year, is not shown on the map.

Map Symbols and Time Zones

Europe

		Area sq km	Area sq miles	Population	Capital	Languages	Religions	Currency	Internet link
ALBANIA		28 748	11 100	3 190 000	Tirana	Albanian, Greek	Sunni Muslim, Albanian Orthodox, Roman Catholic	Lek	www.km.gov.al
ANDORRA		465	180	75 000	Andorra la Vella	Spanish, Catalan, French	Roman Catholic	Euro	www.andorra.ad
AUSTRIA		83 855	32 377	8 361 000	Vienna	German, Croatian, Turkish	Roman Catholic, Protestant	Euro	www.oesterreich.at
BELARUS		207 600	80 155	9 689 000	Minsk	Belorussian, Russian	Belorussian Orthodox, Roman Catholic	Belarus rouble	www.government.by
BELGIUM		30 520	11 784	10 457 000	Brussels	Dutch (Flemish), French (Walloon), German	Roman Catholic, Protestant	Euro	www.belgium.be
BOSNIA-HERZEGOVINA		51 130	19 741	3 935 000	Sarajevo	Bosnian, Serbian, Croatian	Sunni Muslim, Serbian Orthodox, Roman Catholic, Protestant	Marka	www.fbihvlada.gov.ba
BULGARIA		110 994	42 855	7 639 000	Sofia	Bulgarian, Turkish, Romany, Macedonian	Bulgarian Orthodox, Sunni Muslim	Lev	www.government.bg
CROATIA		56 538	21 829	4 555 000	Zagreb	Croatian, Serbian	Roman Catholic, Serbian Orthodox, Sunni Muslim	Kuna	www.vlada.hr
CZECH REPUBLIC		78 864	30 450	10 186 000	Prague	Czech, Moravian, Slovak	Roman Catholic, Protestant	Czech koruna	www.czechcentrum.cz
DENMARK		43 075	16 631	5 442 000	Copenhagen	Danish	Protestant	Danish krone	www.denmark.dk
ESTONIA		45 200	17 452	1 335 000	Tallinn	Estonian, Russian	Protestant, Estonian and Russian Orthodox	Kroon	www.valitsus.ee
FINLAND		338 145	130 559	5 277 000	Helsinki	Finnish, Swedish	Protestant, Greek Orthodox	Euro	www.valtioneuvosto.fi
FRANCE		543 965	210 026	61 647 000	Paris	French, Arabic	Roman Catholic, Protestant, Sunni Muslim	Euro	www.premier-ministre.gouv.fr
GERMANY		357 022	137 849	82 599 000	Berlin	German, Turkish	Protestant, Roman Catholic	Euro	www.bundesregierung.de
GREECE		131 957	50 949	11 147 000	Athens	Greek	Greek Orthodox, Sunni Muslim	Euro	www.greece.gov.gr
HUNGARY		93 030	35 919	10 030 000	Budapest	Hungarian	Roman Catholic, Protestant	Forint	www.magyarorszag.hu
ICELAND		102 820	39 699	301 000	Reykjavík	Icelandic	Protestant	Icelandic króna	www.iceland.is
IRELAND		70 282	27 136	4 301 000	Dublin	English, Irish	Roman Catholic, Protestant	Euro	www.irlgov.ie
ITALY		301 245	116 311	58 877 000	Rome	Italian	Roman Catholic	Euro	www.governo.it
KOSOVO		10 908	4 212	2 070 000	Prishtinë	Albanian, Serbian	Sunni Muslim, Serbian Orthodox	Euro	www.ks-gov.net
LATVIA		63 700	24 595	2 277 000	Rīga	Latvian, Russian	Protestant, Roman Catholic, Russian Orthodox	Lats	www.saeima.lv
LIECHTENSTEIN		160	62	35 000	Vaduz	German	Roman Catholic, Protestant	Swiss franc	www.liechtenstein.li
LITHUANIA		65 200	25 174	3 390 000	Vilnius	Lithuanian, Russian, Polish	Roman Catholic, Protestant, Russian Orthodox	Litas	www.lrv.lt
LUXEMBOURG		2 586	998	467 000	Luxembourg	Letzeburgish, German, French	Roman Catholic	Euro	www.gouvernement.lu
MACEDONIA (F.Y.R.O.M.)		25 713	9 928	2 038 000	Skopje	Macedonian, Albanian, Turkish	Macedonian Orthodox, Sunni Muslim	Macedonian denar	www.vlada.mk
MALTA		316	122	407 000	Valletta	Maltese, English	Roman Catholic	Euro	www.gov.mt
MOLDOVA		33 700	13 012	3 794 000	Chişinău	Romanian, Ukrainian, Gagauz, Russian	Romanian Orthodox, Russian Orthodox	Moldovan leu	www.moldova.md
MONACO		2	1	33 000	Monaco-Ville	French, Monegasque, Italian	Roman Catholic	Euro	www.visitmonaco.com
MONTENEGRO		13 812	5 333	598 000	Podgorica	Serbian (Montenegrin), Albanian	Montenegrin Orthodox, Sunni Muslim	Euro	www.montenegro.yu
NETHERLANDS		41 526	16 033	16 419 000	Amsterdam/The Hague	Dutch, Frisian	Roman Catholic, Protestant, Sunni Muslim	Euro	www.overheid.nl
NORWAY		323 878	125 050	4 698 000	Oslo	Norwegian	Protestant, Roman Catholic	Norwegian krone	www.norway.no
POLAND		312 683	120 728	38 082 000	Warsaw	Polish, German	Roman Catholic, Polish Orthodox	Złoty	www.poland.gov.pl
PORTUGAL		88 940	34 340	10 623 000	Lisbon	Portuguese	Roman Catholic, Protestant	Euro	www.portugal.gov.pt
ROMANIA		237 500	91 699	21 438 000	Bucharest	Romanian, Hungarian	Romanian Orthodox, Protestant, Roman Catholic	Romanian leu	www.guv.ro
RUSSIAN FEDERATION		17 075 400	6 592 849	142 499 000	Moscow	Russian, Tatar, Ukrainian, local languages	Russian Orthodox, Sunni Muslim, Protestant	Russian rouble	www.gov.ru
SAN MARINO		61	24	31 000	San Marino	Italian	Roman Catholic	Euro	www.consigliograndeegenerale.sm
SERBIA		77 453	29 904	7 778 000	Belgrade	Serbian, Hungarian	Serbian Orthodox, Roman Catholic, Sunni Muslim	Serbian dinar,	www.srbija.sr.gov.yu
SLOVAKIA		49 035	18 933	5 390 000	Bratislava	Slovak, Hungarian, Czech	Roman Catholic, Protestant, Orthodox	Euro	www.government.gov.sk
SLOVENIA		20 251	7 819	2 002 000	Ljubljana	Slovene, Croatian, Serbian	Roman Catholic, Protestant	Euro	www.sigov.si
SPAIN		504 782	194 897	44 279 000	Madrid	Castilian, Catalan, Galician, Basque	Roman Catholic	Euro	www.la-moncloa.es
SWEDEN		449 964	173 732	9 119 000	Stockholm	Swedish	Protestant, Roman Catholic	Swedish krona	www.sweden.se
SWITZERLAND		41 293	15 943	7 484 000	Bern	German, French, Italian, Romansch	Roman Catholic, Protestant	Swiss franc	www.admin.ch
UKRAINE		603 700	233 090	46 205 000	Kiev	Ukrainian, Russian	Ukrainian Orthodox, Ukrainian Catholic, Roman Catholic	Hryvnia	www.kmu.gov.ua
UNITED KINGDOM		243 609	94 058	60 769 000	London	English, Welsh, Gaelic	Protestant, Roman Catholic, Muslim	Pound sterling	www.direct.gov.uk
VATICAN CITY		0.5	0.2	557	Vatican City	Italian	Roman Catholic	Euro	www.vatican.va

Asia

		Area sq km	Area sq miles	Population	Capital	Languages	Religions	Currency	Internet link
AFGHANISTAN		652 225	251 825	27 145 000	Kābul	Dari, Pushtu, Uzbek, Turkmen	Sunni Muslim, Shi'a Muslim	Afghani	www.afghanistan-mfa.net
ARMENIA		29 800	11 506	3 002 000	Yerevan	Armenian, Azeri	Armenian Orthodox	Dram	www.gov.am
AZERBAIJAN		86 600	33 436	8 467 000	Baku	Azeri, Armenian, Russian, Lezgian	Shi'a Muslim, Sunni Muslim, Russian and Armenian Orthodox	Azerbaijani manat	www.president.az
BAHRAIN		691	267	753 000	Manama	Arabic, English	Shi'a Muslim, Sunni Muslim, Christian	Bahrain dinar	www.bahrain.gov.bh
BANGLADESH		143 998	55 598	158 665 000	Dhaka	Bengali, English	Sunni Muslim, Hindu	Taka	www.bangladesh.gov.bd
BHUTAN		46 620	18 000	658 000	Thimphu	Dzongkha, Nepali, Assamese	Buddhist, Hindu	Ngultrum, Indian rupee	www.bhutan.gov.bt
BRUNEI		5 765	2 226	390 000	Bandar Seri Begawan	Malay, English, Chinese	Sunni Muslim, Buddhist, Christian	Brunei dollar	www.brunei.gov.bn
CAMBODIA		181 035	69 884	14 444 000	Phnom Penh	Khmer, Vietnamese	Buddhist, Roman Catholic, Sunni Muslim	Riel	www.cambodia.gov.kh
CHINA		9 584 492	3 700 593	1 313 437 000	Beijing	Mandarin, Wu, Cantonese, Hsiang, regional languages	Confucian, Taoist, Buddhist, Christian, Sunni Muslim	Yuan, HK dollar*, Macau pataca	www.china.org.cn
CYPRUS		9 251	3 572	855 000	Nicosia	Greek, Turkish, English	Greek Orthodox, Sunni Muslim	Euro	www.cyprus.gov.cy
EAST TIMOR		14 874	5 743	1 155 000	Dili	Portuguese, Tetun, English	Roman Catholic	United States dollar	www.timor-leste.gov.tl
GEORGIA		69 700	26 911	4 395 000	T'bilisi	Georgian, Russian, Armenian, Azeri, Ossetian, Abkhaz	Georgian Orthodox, Russian Orthodox, Sunni Muslim	Lari	www.parliament.ge
INDIA		3 064 898	1 183 364	1 169 016 000	New Delhi	Hindi, English, many regional languages	Hindu, Sunni Muslim, Shi'a Muslim, Sikh, Christian	Indian rupee	www.india.gov.in
INDONESIA		1 919 445	741 102	231 627 000	Jakarta	Indonesian, local languages	Sunni Muslim, Protestant, Roman Catholic, Hindu, Buddhist	Rupiah	www.indonesia.go.id
IRAN		1 648 000	636 296	71 208 000	Tehrān	Farsi, Azeri, Kurdish, regional languages	Shi'a Muslim, Sunni Muslim	Iranian rial	www.president.ir
IRAQ		438 317	169 235	28 993 000	Baghdād	Arabic, Kurdish, Turkmen	Shi'a Muslim, Sunni Muslim, Christian	Iraqi dinar	www.iraqigovernment.org
ISRAEL		20 770	8 019	6 928 000	Jerusalem (Yerushalayim) (El Quds)**	Hebrew, Arabic	Jewish, Sunni Muslim, Christian, Druze	Shekel	www.gov.il
JAPAN		377 727	145 841	127 967 000	Tōkyō	Japanese	Shintoist, Buddhist, Christian	Yen	web-japan.org
JORDAN		89 206	34 443	5 924 000	'Ammān	Arabic	Sunni Muslim, Christian	Jordanian dinar	www.jordan.jo
KAZAKHSTAN		2 717 300	1 049 155	15 422 000	Astana	Kazakh, Russian, Ukrainian, German, Uzbek, Tatar	Sunni Muslim, Russian Orthodox, Protestant	Tenge	www.government.kz
KUWAIT		17 818	6 880	2 851 000	Kuwait	Arabic	Sunni Muslim, Shi'a Muslim, Christian, Hindu	Kuwaiti dinar	www.e.gov.kw
KYRGYZSTAN		198 500	76 641	5 317 000	Bishkek	Kyrgyz, Russian, Uzbek	Sunni Muslim, Russian Orthodox	Kyrgyz som	www.gov.kg
LAOS		236 800	91 429	5 859 000	Vientiane	Lao, local languages	Buddhist, traditional beliefs	Kip	www.un.int/lao
LEBANON		10 452	4 036	4 099 000	Beirut	Arabic, Armenian, French	Shi'a Muslim, Sunni Muslim, Christian	Lebanese pound	www.presidency.gov.lb
MALAYSIA		332 965	128 559	26 572 000	Kuala Lumpur/Putrajaya	Malay, English, Chinese, Tamil, local languages	Sunni Muslim, Buddhist, Hindu, Christian, traditional beliefs	Ringgit	www.gov.my

**De facto capital. Disputed   *Hong Kong dollar

		Area sq km	Area sq miles	Population	Capital	Languages	Religions	Currency	Internet link
MALDIVES		298	115	306 000	Male	Divehi (Maldivian)	Sunni Muslim	Rufiyaa	www.maldivesinfo.gov.mv
MONGOLIA		1 565 000	604 250	2 629 000	Ulan Bator	Khalka (Mongolian), Kazakh, local languages	Buddhist, Sunni Muslim	Tugrik (tögrög)	www.pmis.gov.mn
MYANMAR (BURMA)		676 577	261 228	48 798 000	Nay Pyi Taw/Rangoon	Burmese, Shan, Karen, local languages	Buddhist, Christian, Sunni Muslim	Kyat	www.myanmar.com
NEPAL		147 181	56 827	28 196 000	Kathmandu	Nepali, Maithili, Bhojpuri, English, local languages	Hindu, Buddhist, Sunni Muslim	Nepalese rupee	www.nepalhmg.gov.np
NORTH KOREA		120 538	46 540	23 790 000	P'yŏngyang	Korean	Traditional beliefs, Chondoist, Buddhist	North Korean won	www.korea-dpr.com
OMAN		309 500	119 499	2 595 000	Muscat	Arabic, Baluchi, Indian languages	Ibadhi Muslim, Sunni Muslim	Omani riyal	www.omanet.om
PAKISTAN		803 940	310 403	163 902 000	Islamabad	Urdu, Punjabi, Sindhi, Pushtu, English	Sunni Muslim, Shi'a Muslim, Christian, Hindu	Pakistani rupee	www.infopak.gov.pk
PALAU		497	192	20 000	Melekeok	Palauan, English	Roman Catholic, Protestant, traditional beliefs	United States dollar	www.palauembassy.com
PHILIPPINES		300 000	115 831	87 960 000	Manila	English, Filipino, Tagalog, Cebuano, local languages	Roman Catholic, Protestant, Sunni Muslim, Aglipayan	Philippine peso	www.gov.ph
QATAR		11 437	4 416	841 000	Doha	Arabic	Sunni Muslim	Qatari riyal	www.mofa.gov.qa
RUSSIAN FEDERATION		17 075 400	6 592 849	142 499 000	Moscow	Russian, Tatar, Ukrainian, local languages	Russian Orthodox, Sunni Muslim, Protestant	Russian rouble	www.gov.ru
SAUDI ARABIA		2 200 000	849 425	24 735 000	Riyadh	Arabic	Sunni Muslim, Shi'a Muslim	Saudi Arabian riyal	www.saudinf.com
SINGAPORE		639	247	4 436 000	Singapore	Chinese, English, Malay, Tamil	Buddhist, Taoist, Sunni Muslim, Christian, Hindu	Singapore dollar	www.gov.sg
SOUTH KOREA		99 274	38 330	48 224 000	Seoul	Korean	Buddhist, Protestant, Roman Catholic	South Korean won	www.korea.net
SRI LANKA		65 610	25 332	19 299 000	Sri Jayewardenepura Kotte	Sinhalese, Tamil, English	Buddhist, Hindu, Sunni Muslim, Roman Catholic	Sri Lankan rupee	www.priu.gov.lk
SYRIA		185 180	71 498	19 929 000	Damascus	Arabic, Kurdish, Armenian	Sunni Muslim, Shi'a Muslim, Christian	Syrian pound	www.moi-syria.com
TAIWAN		36 179	13 969	22 880 000	T'aipei	Mandarin, Min, Hakka, local languages	Buddhist, Taoist, Confucian, Christian	Taiwan dollar	www.gov.tw
TAJIKISTAN		143 100	55 251	6 736 000	Dushanbe	Tajik, Uzbek, Russian	Sunni Muslim	Somoni	www.tjus.org
THAILAND		513 115	198 115	63 884 000	Bangkok	Thai, Lao, Chinese, Malay, Mon-Khmer languages	Buddhist, Sunni Muslim	Baht	www.thaigov.go.th
TURKEY		779 452	300 948	74 877 000	Ankara	Turkish, Kurdish	Sunni Muslim, Shi'a Muslim	Lira	www.mfa.gov.tr
TURKMENISTAN		488 100	188 456	4 965 000	Aşgabat	Turkmen, Uzbek, Russian	Sunni Muslim, Russian Orthodox	Turkmen manat	www.turkmenistanembassy.org
UNITED ARAB EMIRATES		77 700	30 000	4 380 000	Abu Dhabi	Arabic, English	Sunni Muslim, Shi'a Muslim	United Arab Emirates dirham	www.uae.gov.ae
UZBEKISTAN		447 400	172 742	27 372 000	Toshkent	Uzbek, Russian, Tajik, Kazakh	Sunni Muslim, Russian Orthodox	Uzbek som	www.gov.uz
VIETNAM		329 565	127 246	87 375 000	Ha Nôi	Vietnamese, Thai, Khmer, Chinese, local languages	Buddhist, Taoist, Roman Catholic, Cao Dai, Hoa Hao	Dong	www.na.gov.vn
YEMEN		527 968	203 850	22 389 000	Şan'ã'	Arabic	Sunni Muslim, Shi'a Muslim	Yemeni rial	www.nic.gov.ye

Africa

		Area sq km	Area sq miles	Population	Capital	Languages	Religions	Currency	Internet link
ALGERIA		2 381 741	919 595	33 858 000	Algiers	Arabic, French, Berber	Sunni Muslim	Algerian dinar	www.el-mouradia.dz
ANGOLA		1 246 700	481 354	17 024 000	Luanda	Portuguese, Bantu, local languages	Roman Catholic, Protestant, traditional beliefs	Kwanza	www.angola.org
BENIN		112 620	43 483	9 033 000	Porto-Novo	French, Fon, Yoruba, Adja, local languages	Traditional beliefs, Roman Catholic, Sunni Muslim	CFA franc*	www.gouv.bj/en/index.php
BOTSWANA		581 370	224 468	1 882 000	Gaborone	English, Setswana, Shona, local languages	Traditional beliefs, Protestant, Roman Catholic	Pula	www.gov.bw
BURKINA		274 200	105 869	14 784 000	Ouagadougou	French, Moore (Mossi), Fulani, local languages	Sunni Muslim, traditional beliefs, Roman Catholic	CFA franc*	www.primature.gov.bf
BURUNDI		27 835	10 747	8 508 000	Bujumbura	Kirundi (Hutu, Tutsi), French	Roman Catholic, traditional beliefs, Protestant	Burundian franc	www.burundi.gov.bi
CAMEROON		475 442	183 569	18 549 000	Yaoundé	French, English, Fang, Bamileke, local languages	Roman Catholic, traditional beliefs, Sunni Muslim, Protestant	CFA franc*	www.spm.gov.cm
CAPE VERDE		4 033	1 557	530 000	Praia	Portuguese, creole	Roman Catholic, Protestant	Cape Verde escudo	www.governo.cv
CENTRAL AFRICAN REPUBLIC		622 436	240 324	4 343 000	Bangui	French, Sango, Banda, Baya, local languages	Protestant, Roman Catholic, traditional beliefs, Sunni Muslim	CFA franc*	www.rca-gouv.org
CHAD		1 284 000	495 755	10 781 000	Ndjamena	Arabic, French, Sara, local languages	Sunni Muslim, Roman Catholic, Protestant, traditional beliefs	CFA franc*	www.primature-tchad.org
COMOROS		1 862	719	839 000	Moroni	Comorian, French, Arabic	Sunni Muslim, Roman Catholic	Comoros franc	www.beit-salam.km
CONGO		342 000	132 047	3 768 000	Brazzaville	French, Kongo, Monokutuba, local languages	Roman Catholic, Protestant, traditional beliefs, Sunni Muslim	CFA franc*	www.congo-site.com
CONGO, DEM. REP. OF THE		2 345 410	905 568	62 636 000	Kinshasa	French, Lingala, Swahili, Kongo, local languages	Christian, Sunni Muslim	Congolese franc	www.un.int/drcongo
CÔTE D'IVOIRE (IVORY COAST)		322 463	124 504	19 262 000	Yamoussoukro	French, creole, Akan, local languages	Sunni Muslim, Roman Catholic, traditional beliefs, Protestant	CFA franc*	www.presidence.ci
DJIBOUTI		23 200	8 958	833 000	Djibouti	Somali, Afar, French, Arabic	Sunni Muslim, Christian	Djibouti franc	www.presidence.dj
EGYPT		1 000 250	386 199	75 498 000	Cairo	Arabic	Sunni Muslim, Coptic Christian	Egyptian pound	www.sis.gov.eg
EQUATORIAL GUINEA		28 051	10 831	507 000	Malabo	Spanish, French, Fang	Roman Catholic, traditional beliefs	CFA franc*	www.ceiba-equatorial-guinea.org
ERITREA		117 400	45 328	4 851 000	Asmara	Tigrinya, Tigre	Sunni Muslim, Coptic Christian	Nakfa	shabait.com
ETHIOPIA		1 133 880	437 794	83 099 000	Addis Ababa	Oromo, Amharic, Tigrinya, local languages	Ethiopian Orthodox, Sunni Muslim, traditional beliefs	Birr	www.ethiopar.net
GABON		267 667	103 347	1 331 000	Libreville	French, Fang, local languages	Roman Catholic, Protestant, traditional beliefs	CFA franc*	www.legabon.org
THE GAMBIA		11 295	4 361	1 709 000	Banjul	English, Malinke, Fulani, Wolof	Sunni Muslim, Protestant	Dalasi	www.statehouse.gm
GHANA		238 537	92 100	23 478 000	Accra	English, Hausa, Akan, local languages	Christian, Sunni Muslim, traditional beliefs	Cedi	www.ghana.gov.gh
GUINEA		245 857	94 926	9 370 000	Conakry	French, Fulani, Malinke, local languages	Sunni Muslim, traditional beliefs, Christian	Guinea franc	www.guinee.gov.gn
GUINEA-BISSAU		36 125	13 948	1 695 000	Bissau	Portuguese, crioulo, local languages	Traditional beliefs, Sunni Muslim, Christian	CFA franc*	www.republica-da-guine-bissau.org
KENYA		582 646	224 961	37 538 000	Nairobi	Swahili, English, local languages	Christian, traditional beliefs	Kenyan shilling	www.kenya.go.ke
LESOTHO		30 355	11 720	2 008 000	Maseru	Sesotho, English, Zulu	Christian, traditional beliefs	Loti, S. African rand	www.lesotho.gov.ls
LIBERIA		111 369	43 000	3 750 000	Monrovia	English, creole, local languages	Traditional beliefs, Christian, Sunni Muslim	Liberian dollar	www.micat.gov.lr
LIBYA		1 759 540	679 362	6 160 000	Tripoli	Arabic, Berber	Sunni Muslim	Libyan dinar	
MADAGASCAR		587 041	226 658	19 683 000	Antananarivo	Malagasy, French	Traditional beliefs, Christian, Sunni Muslim	Malagasy Ariary, Malagasy franc	www.madagascar.gov.mg
MALAWI		118 484	45 747	13 925 000	Lilongwe	Chichewa, English, local languages	Christian, traditional beliefs, Sunni Muslim	Malawian kwacha	www.malawi.gov.mw
MALI		1 240 140	478 821	12 337 000	Bamako	French, Bambara, local languages	Sunni Muslim, traditional beliefs, Christian	CFA franc*	www.maliensdelexterieur.gov.ml
MAURITANIA		1 030 700	397 955	3 124 000	Nouakchott	Arabic, French, local languages	Sunni Muslim	Ouguiya	www.mauritania.mr
MAURITIUS		2 040	788	1 262 000	Port Louis	English, creole, Hindi, Bhojpurī, French	Hindu, Roman Catholic, Sunni Muslim	Mauritius rupee	www.gov.mu
MOROCCO		446 550	172 414	31 224 000	Rabat	Arabic, Berber, French	Sunni Muslim	Moroccan dirham	www.maroc.ma
MOZAMBIQUE		799 380	308 642	21 397 000	Maputo	Portuguese, Makua, Tsonga, local languages	Traditional beliefs, Roman Catholic, Sunni Muslim	Metical	www.mozambique.mz
NAMIBIA		824 292	318 261	2 074 000	Windhoek	English, Afrikaans, German, Ovambo, local languages	Protestant, Roman Catholic	Namibian dollar	www.grnnet.gov.na
NIGER		1 267 000	489 191	14 226 000	Niamey	French, Hausa, Fulani, local languages	Sunni Muslim, traditional beliefs	CFA franc*	www.delgi.ne/presidence
NIGERIA		923 768	356 669	148 093 000	Abuja	English, Hausa, Yoruba, Ibo, Fulani, local languages	Sunni Muslim, Christian, traditional beliefs	Naira	www.nigeria.gov.ng
RWANDA		26 338	10 169	9 725 000	Kigali	Kinyarwanda, French, English	Roman Catholic, traditional beliefs, Protestant	Rwandan franc	www.gov.rw
SÃO TOMÉ AND PRÍNCIPE		964	372	158 000	São Tomé	Portuguese, creole	Roman Catholic, Protestant	Dobra	www.parlamento.st
SENEGAL		196 720	75 954	12 379 000	Dakar	French, Wolof, Fulani, local languages	Sunni Muslim, Roman Catholic, traditional beliefs	CFA franc*	www.gouv.sn

*Communauté Financière Africaine franc

Africa continued

		Area sq km	Area sq miles	Population	Capital	Languages	Religions	Currency	Internet link
SEYCHELLES		455	176	87 000	Victoria	English, French, creole	Roman Catholic, Protestant	Seychelles rupee	www.virtualseychelles.sc
SIERRA LEONE		71 740	27 699	5 866 000	Freetown	English, creole, Mende, Temne, local languages	Sunni Muslim, traditional beliefs	Leone	www.statehouse-sl.org
SOMALIA		637 657	246 201	8 699 000	Mogadishu	Somali, Arabic	Sunni Muslim	Somali shilling	www.somali-gov.info
SOUTH AFRICA, REPUBLIC OF		1 219 090	470 693	48 577 000	Pretoria/Cape Town	Afrikaans, English, nine official local languages	Protestant, Roman Catholic, Sunni Muslim, Hindu	Rand	www.gov.za
SUDAN		2 505 813	967 500	38 560 000	Khartoum	Arabic, Dinka, Nubian, Beja, Nuer, local languages	Sunni Muslim, traditional beliefs, Christian	Sudanese pound (Sudani)	www.sudan.gov.sd
SWAZILAND		17 364	6 704	1 141 000	Mbabane	Swazi, English	Christian, traditional beliefs	Emalangeni, South African rand	www.gov.sz
TANZANIA		945 087	364 900	40 454 000	Dodoma	Swahili, English, Nyamwezi, local languages	Shi'a Muslim, Sunni Muslim, traditional beliefs, Christian	Tanzanian shilling	www.tanzania.go.tz
TOGO		56 785	21 925	6 585 000	Lomé	French, Ewe, Kabre, local languages	Traditional beliefs, Christian, Sunni Muslim	CFA franc*	www.republicoftogo.com
TUNISIA		164 150	63 379	10 327 000	Tunis	Arabic, French	Sunni Muslim	Tunisian dinar	www.tunisiaonline.com
UGANDA		241 038	93 065	30 884 000	Kampala	English, Swahili, Luganda, local languages	Roman Catholic, Protestant, Sunni Muslim, traditional beliefs	Ugandan shilling	www.mofa.go.ug
ZAMBIA		752 614	290 586	11 922 000	Lusaka	English, Bemba, Nyanja, Tonga, local languages	Christian, traditional beliefs	Zambian kwacha	www.statehouse.gov.zm
ZIMBABWE		390 759	150 873	13 349 000	Harare	English, Shona, Ndebele	Christian, traditional beliefs	Zimbabwean dollar	www.zim.gov.zw

*Communauté Financière Africaine franc

Oceania

		Area sq km	Area sq miles	Population	Capital	Languages	Religions	Currency	Internet link
AUSTRALIA		7 692 024	2 969 907	20 743 000	Canberra	English, Italian, Greek	Protestant, Roman Catholic, Orthodox	Australian dollar	www.gov.au
FIJI		18 330	7 077	839 000	Suva	English, Fijian, Hindi	Christian, Hindu, Sunni Muslim	Fiji dollar	www.fiji.gov.fj
KIRIBATI		717	277	95 000	Bairiki	Gilbertese, English	Roman Catholic, Protestant	Australian dollar	
MARSHALL ISLANDS		181	70	59 000	Delap-Uliga-Djarrit	English, Marshallese	Protestant, Roman Catholic	United States dollar	www.rmiembassyus.org
MICRONESIA, FEDERATED STATES OF		701	271	111 000	Palikir	English, Chuukese, Pohnpeian, local languages	Roman Catholic, Protestant	United States dollar	fsmgov.org
NAURU		21	8	10 000	Yaren	Nauruan, English	Protestant, Roman Catholic	Australian dollar	www.un.int/nauru
NEW ZEALAND		270 534	104 454	4 179 000	Wellington	English, Maori	Protestant, Roman Catholic	New Zealand dollar	www.govt.nz
PAPUA NEW GUINEA		462 840	178 704	6 331 000	Port Moresby	English, Tok Pisin (creole), local languages	Protestant, Roman Catholic, traditional beliefs	Kina	www.pngonline.gov.pg
SAMOA		2 831	1 093	187 000	Apia	Samoan, English	Protestant, Roman Catholic	Tala	www.govt.ws
SOLOMON ISLANDS		28 370	10 954	496 000	Honiara	English, creole, local languages	Protestant, Roman Catholic	Solomon Islands dollar	www.commerce.gov.sb
TONGA		748	289	100 000	Nuku'alofa	Tongan, English	Protestant, Roman Catholic	Pa'anga	www.pmo.gov.to
TUVALU		25	10	11 000	Vaiaku	Tuvaluan, English	Protestant	Australian dollar	
VANUATU		12 190	4 707	226 000	Port Vila	English, Bislama (creole), French	Protestant, Roman Catholic, traditional beliefs	Vatu	www.vanuatugovernment.gov.vu

North America

		Area sq km	Area sq miles	Population	Capital	Languages	Religions	Currency	Internet link
ANTIGUA AND BARBUDA		442	171	85 000	St John's	English, creole	Protestant, Roman Catholic	East Caribbean dollar	www.ab.gov.ag
THE BAHAMAS		13 939	5 382	331 000	Nassau	English, creole	Protestant, Roman Catholic	Bahamian dollar	www.bahamas.gov.bs
BARBADOS		430	166	294 000	Bridgetown	English, creole	Protestant, Roman Catholic	Barbados dollar	www.barbados.gov.bb
BELIZE		22 965	8 867	288 000	Belmopan	English, Spanish, Mayan, creole	Roman Catholic, Protestant	Belize dollar	www.belize.gov.bz
CANADA		9 984 670	3 855 103	32 876 000	Ottawa	English, French, local languages	Roman Catholic, Protestant, Eastern Orthodox, Jewish	Canadian dollar	canada.gc.ca
COSTA RICA		51 100	19 730	4 468 000	San José	Spanish	Roman Catholic, Protestant	Costa Rican colón	www.casapres.go.cr
CUBA		110 860	42 803	11 268 000	Havana	Spanish	Roman Catholic, Protestant	Cuban peso	www.cubagob.gov.cu
DOMINICA		750	290	67 000	Roseau	English, creole	Roman Catholic, Protestant	East Caribbean dollar	www.ndcdominica.dm
DOMINICAN REPUBLIC		48 442	18 704	9 760 000	Santo Domingo	Spanish, creole	Roman Catholic, Protestant	Dominican peso	www.cig.gov.do
EL SALVADOR		21 041	8 124	6 857 000	San Salvador	Spanish	Roman Catholic, Protestant	El Salvador colón, United States dollar	www.casapres.gob.sv
GRENADA		378	146	106 000	St George's	English, creole	Roman Catholic, Protestant	East Caribbean dollar	www.gov.gd
GUATEMALA		108 890	42 043	13 354 000	Guatemala City	Spanish, Mayan languages	Roman Catholic, Protestant	Quetzal, United States dollar	www.congreso.gob.gt
HAITI		27 750	10 714	9 598 000	Port-au-Prince	French, creole	Roman Catholic, Protestant, Voodoo	Gourde	www.haiti.org
HONDURAS		112 088	43 277	7 106 000	Tegucigalpa	Spanish, Amerindian languages	Roman Catholic, Protestant	Lempira	www.congreso.gob.hn
JAMAICA		10 991	4 244	2 714 000	Kingston	English, creole	Protestant, Roman Catholic	Jamaican dollar	www.jis.gov.jm
MEXICO		1 972 545	761 604	106 535 000	Mexico City	Spanish, Amerindian languages	Roman Catholic, Protestant	Mexican peso	www.gob.mx
NICARAGUA		130 000	50 193	5 603 000	Managua	Spanish, Amerindian languages	Roman Catholic, Protestant	Córdoba	www.asamblea.gob.ni
PANAMA		77 082	29 762	3 343 000	Panama City	Spanish, English, Amerindian languages	Roman Catholic, Protestant, Sunni Muslim	Balboa	www.pa
ST KITTS AND NEVIS		261	101	50 000	Basseterre	English, creole	Protestant, Roman Catholic	East Caribbean dollar	www.gov.kn
ST LUCIA		616	238	165 000	Castries	English, creole	Roman Catholic, Protestant	East Caribbean dollar	www.stlucia.gov.lc
ST VINCENT AND THE GRENADINES		389	150	120 000	Kingstown	English, creole	Protestant, Roman Catholic	East Caribbean dollar	
TRINIDAD AND TOBAGO		5 130	1 981	1 333 000	Port of Spain	English, creole, Hindi	Roman Catholic, Hindu, Protestant, Sunni Muslim	Trinidad and Tobago dollar	www.gov.tt
UNITED STATES OF AMERICA		9 826 635	3 794 085	305 826 000	Washington D.C.	English, Spanish	Protestant, Roman Catholic, Sunni Muslim, Jewish	United States dollar	www.firstgov.gov

South America

		Area sq km	Area sq miles	Population	Capital	Languages	Religions	Currency	Internet link
ARGENTINA		2 766 889	1 068 302	39 531 000	Buenos Aires	Spanish, Italian, Amerindian languages	Roman Catholic, Protestant	Argentinian peso	www.info.gov.ar
BOLIVIA		1 098 581	424 164	9 525 000	La Paz/Sucre	Spanish, Quechua, Aymara	Roman Catholic, Protestant, Baha'i	Boliviano	www.bolivia.gov.bo
BRAZIL		8 514 879	3 287 613	191 791 000	Brasília	Portuguese	Roman Catholic, Protestant	Real	www.brazil.gov.br
CHILE		756 945	292 258	16 635 000	Santiago	Spanish, Amerindian languages	Roman Catholic, Protestant	Chilean peso	www.gobiernodechile.cl
COLOMBIA		1 141 748	440 831	46 156 000	Bogotá	Spanish, Amerindian languages	Roman Catholic, Protestant	Colombian peso	www.gobiernoenlinea.gov.co
ECUADOR		272 045	105 037	13 341 000	Quito	Spanish, Quechua, other Amerindian languages	Roman Catholic	US dollar	www.ec-gov.net
GUYANA		214 969	83 000	738 000	Georgetown	English, creole, Amerindian languages	Protestant, Hindu, Roman Catholic, Sunni Muslim	Guyana dollar	www.gina.gov.gy
PARAGUAY		406 752	157 048	6 127 000	Asunción	Spanish, Guaraní	Roman Catholic, Protestant	Guaraní	www.presidencia.gov.py
PERU		1 285 216	496 225	27 903 000	Lima	Spanish, Quechua, Aymara	Roman Catholic, Protestant	Sol	www.peru.gob.pe
SURINAME		163 820	63 251	458 000	Paramaribo	Dutch, Surinamese, English, Hindi	Hindu, Roman Catholic, Protestant, Sunni Muslim	Suriname guilder	www.kabinet.sr.org
URUGUAY		176 215	68 037	3 340 000	Montevideo	Spanish	Roman Catholic, Protestant, Jewish	Uruguayan peso	www.presidencia.gub.uy
VENEZUELA		912 050	352 144	27 657 000	Caracas	Spanish, Amerindian languages	Roman Catholic, Protestant	Bolívar fuerte	www.gobiernoenlinea.ve

The current pattern of the world's countries and territories is a result of a long history of exploration, colonialism, conflict and politics. The fact that there are currently 195 independent countries in the world – the most recent, Kosovo, only being created in February 2008 – illustrates the significant political changes which have occurred since 1950 when there were only eighty-two. There has been a steady progression away from colonial influences over the last fifty years, although many dependent overseas territories remain.

The shapes of countries and the pattern of international boundaries reflect both physical and political processes. Some borders follow natural features – rivers, mountain ranges, etc – others are defined according to political agreement or as a result of war. Some are still subject to dispute between two or more countries, and many remain undefined on the ground.

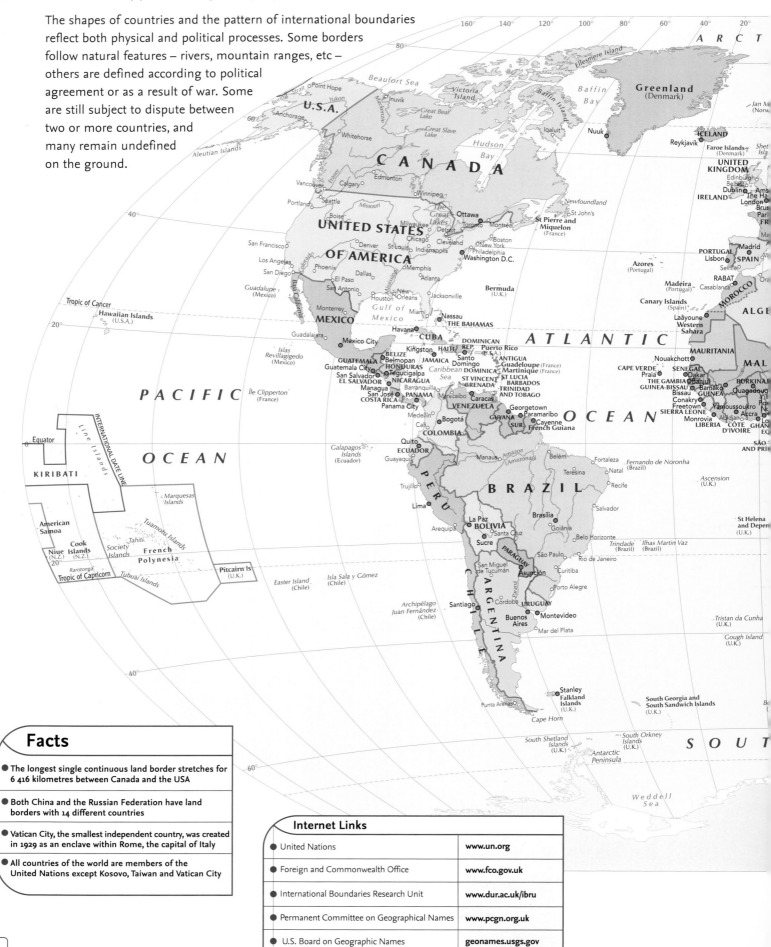

Facts

- The longest single continuous land border stretches for 6 416 kilometres between Canada and the USA
- Both China and the Russian Federation have land borders with 14 different countries
- Vatican City, the smallest independent country, was created in 1929 as an enclave within Rome, the capital of Italy
- All countries of the world are members of the United Nations except Kosovo, Taiwan and Vatican City

Internet Links

United Nations	www.un.org
Foreign and Commonwealth Office	www.fco.gov.uk
International Boundaries Research Unit	www.dur.ac.uk/ibru
Permanent Committee on Geographical Names	www.pcgn.org.uk
U.S. Board on Geographic Names	geonames.usgs.gov

Abbreviation Key

A.	ANDORRA	HUN.	HUNGARY	R.F.	RUSSIAN FEDERATION
AL.	ALBANIA	ISR.	ISRAEL	ROM.	ROMANIA
ARM.	ARMENIA	JOR.	JORDAN	S.	SERBIA
AUST.	AUSTRIA	K.	KOSOVO	SL.	SLOVENIA
AZER.	AZERBAIJAN	L.	LUXEMBOURG	SLA.	SLOVAKIA
B.	BURUNDI	LAT.	LATVIA	SUR.	SURINAME
BE.	BENIN	LEB.	LEBANON	SW.	SWITZERLAND
BEL.	BELGIUM	LITH.	LITHUANIA	T.	TOGO
B.H.	BOSNIA-HERZEGOVINA	M.	MONTENEGRO	TAJIK.	TAJIKISTAN
BULG.	BULGARIA	MA.	MACEDONIA	TURKM.	TURKMENISTAN
CR.	CROATIA	MOL.	MOLDOVA	U.A.E.	UNITED ARAB EMIRATES
CZ.R.	CZECH REPUBLIC	NETH.	NETHERLANDS	U.K.	UNITED KINGDOM
EST.	ESTONIA	N.Z.	NEW ZEALAND	U.S.A.	UNITED STATES OF AMERICA
GEOR.	GEORGIA	R.	RWANDA	UZBEK.	UZBEKISTAN

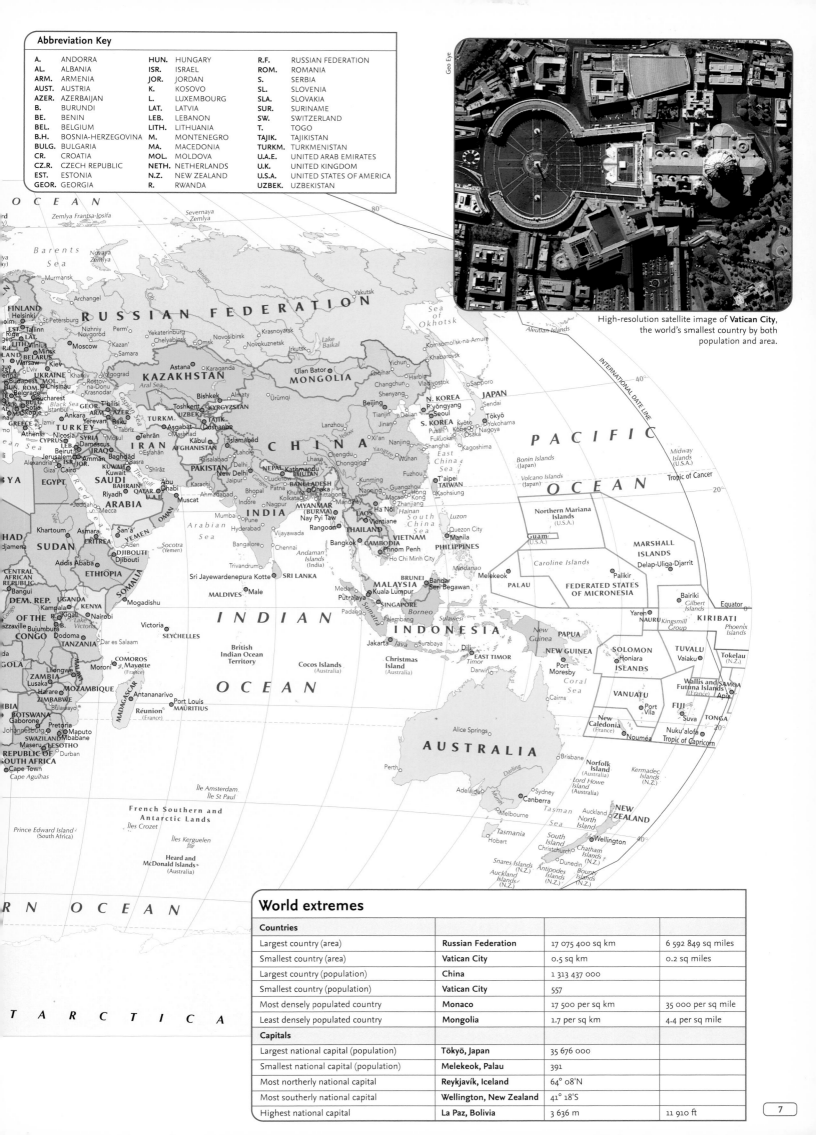

High-resolution satellite image of **Vatican City**, the world's smallest country by both population and area.

World extremes

Countries			
Largest country (area)	**Russian Federation**	17 075 400 sq km	6 592 849 sq miles
Smallest country (area)	**Vatican City**	0.5 sq km	0.2 sq miles
Largest country (population)	**China**	1 313 437 000	
Smallest country (population)	**Vatican City**	557	
Most densely populated country	**Monaco**	17 500 per sq km	35 000 per sq mile
Least densely populated country	**Mongolia**	1.7 per sq km	4.4 per sq mile
Capitals			
Largest national capital (population)	**Tōkyō, Japan**	35 676 000	
Smallest national capital (population)	**Melekeok, Palau**	391	
Most northerly national capital	**Reykjavík, Iceland**	64° 08'N	
Most southerly national capital	**Wellington, New Zealand**	41° 18'S	
Highest national capital	**La Paz, Bolivia**	3 636 m	11 910 ft

World
Landscapes

The earth's physical features, both on land and on the sea bed, closely reflect its geological structure. The current shapes of the continents and oceans have evolved over millions of years. Movements of the tectonic plates which make up the earth's crust have created some of the best-known and most spectacular features. The processes which have shaped the earth continue today with earthquakes, volcanoes, erosion, climatic variations and man's activities all affecting the earth's landscapes.

The total topographic range of the earth's surface is nearly 20 000 metres, from the highest point Mount Everest, to the lowest point in the Mariana Trench. Major mountain ranges include the Himalaya, the Andes and the Rocky Mountains, each of which give rise to some of the world's greatest rivers. In contrast, the deserts of the Sahara, Australia, the Arabian Peninsula and the Gobi cover vast areas and each provide unique landscapes.

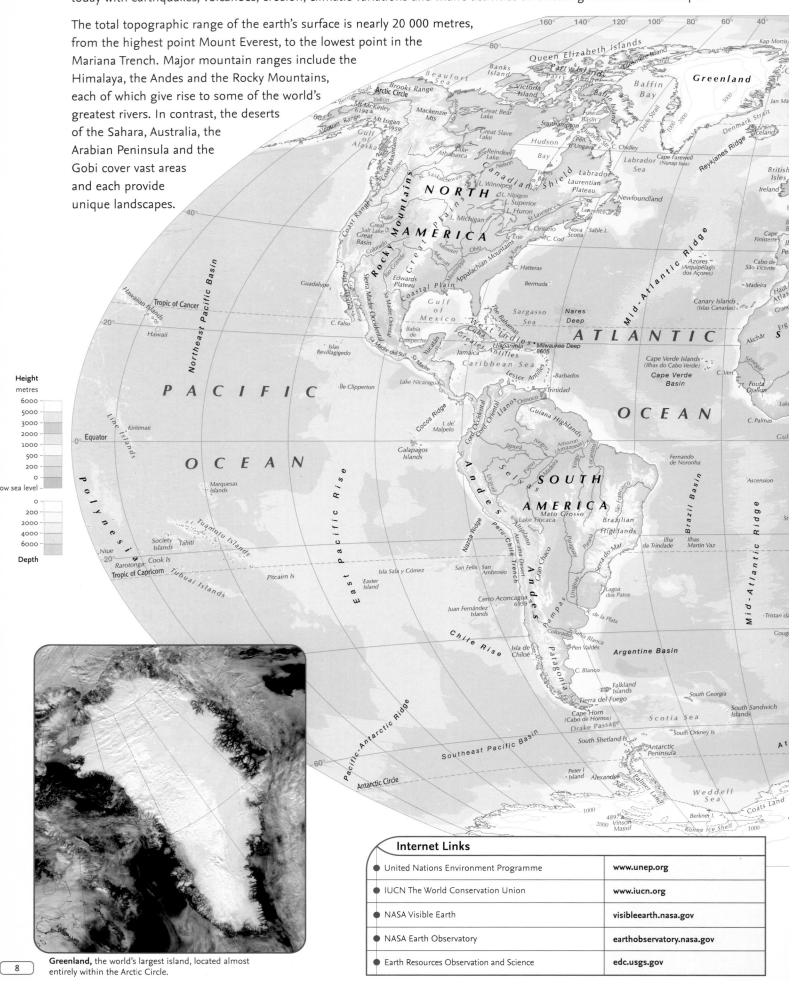

Greenland, the world's largest island, located almost entirely within the Arctic Circle.

Internet Links	
● United Nations Environment Programme	**www.unep.org**
● IUCN The World Conservation Union	**www.iucn.org**
● NASA Visible Earth	**visibleearth.nasa.gov**
● NASA Earth Observatory	**earthobservatory.nasa.gov**
● Earth Resources Observation and Science	**edc.usgs.gov**

Earth's dimensions

Mass	5.974 x 10²¹ tonnes
Total area	509 450 000 sq km / 196 698 645 sq miles
Land area	149 450 000 sq km / 57 702 645 sq miles
Water area	360 000 000 sq km / 138 996 000 sq miles
Volume	1 083 207 x 10⁶ cubic km / 259 911 x 10⁶ cubic miles
Equatorial diameter	12 756 km / 7 927 miles
Polar diameter	12 714 km / 7 901 miles
Equatorial circumference	40 075 km / 24 903 miles
Meridional circumference	40 008 km / 24 861 miles

Mass value corrected: 5.974×10^{21} tonnes; Volume $1\,083\,207 \times 10^{6}$ cubic km / $259\,911 \times 10^{6}$ cubic miles.

Facts

- Approximately 10% of the Earth's land surface is permanently covered by ice
- The Pacific Ocean is larger than all the continents' land areas combined
- The world's highest waterfall, 979 metres high, is Angel Falls, Venezuela
- 52% of the Earth's land surface is below 500 metres
- The mean elevation of the Earth's land surface is 840 metres
- Lake Baikal is the world's deepest lake with a maximum depth of 1 741 metres

World's physical features

Highest mountains			Largest islands		
Mt Everest, China/Nepal	8 848 m	29 028 ft	Greenland, North America	2 175 600 sq km	840 004 sq miles
K2, China/Pakistan	8 611 m	28 251 ft	New Guinea, Oceania	808 510 sq km	312 167 sq miles
Kangchenjunga, India/Nepal	8 586 m	28 169 ft	Borneo, Asia	745 561 sq km	287 863 sq miles
Lhotse, China/Nepal	8 516 m	27 939 ft	Madagascar, Africa	587 040 sq km	226 657 sq miles
Makalu, China/Nepal	8 463 m	27 765 ft	Baffin Island, North America	507 451 sq km	195 927 sq miles
Longest rivers			**Largest lakes**		
Nile, Africa	6 695 km	4 160 miles	Caspian Sea, Asia/Europe	371 000 sq km	143 243 sq miles
Amazon, South America	6 516 km	4 049 miles	Lake Superior, North America	82 100 sq km	31 699 sq miles
Yangtze, Asia	6 380 km	3 965 miles	Lake Victoria, Africa	68 800 sq km	26 564 sq miles
Mississippi-Missouri, North America	5 969 km	3 709 miles	Lake Huron, North America	59 600 sq km	23 012 sq miles
Ob'-Irtysh, Asia	5 568 km	3 460 miles	Lake Michigan, North America	57 800 sq km	22 317 sq miles

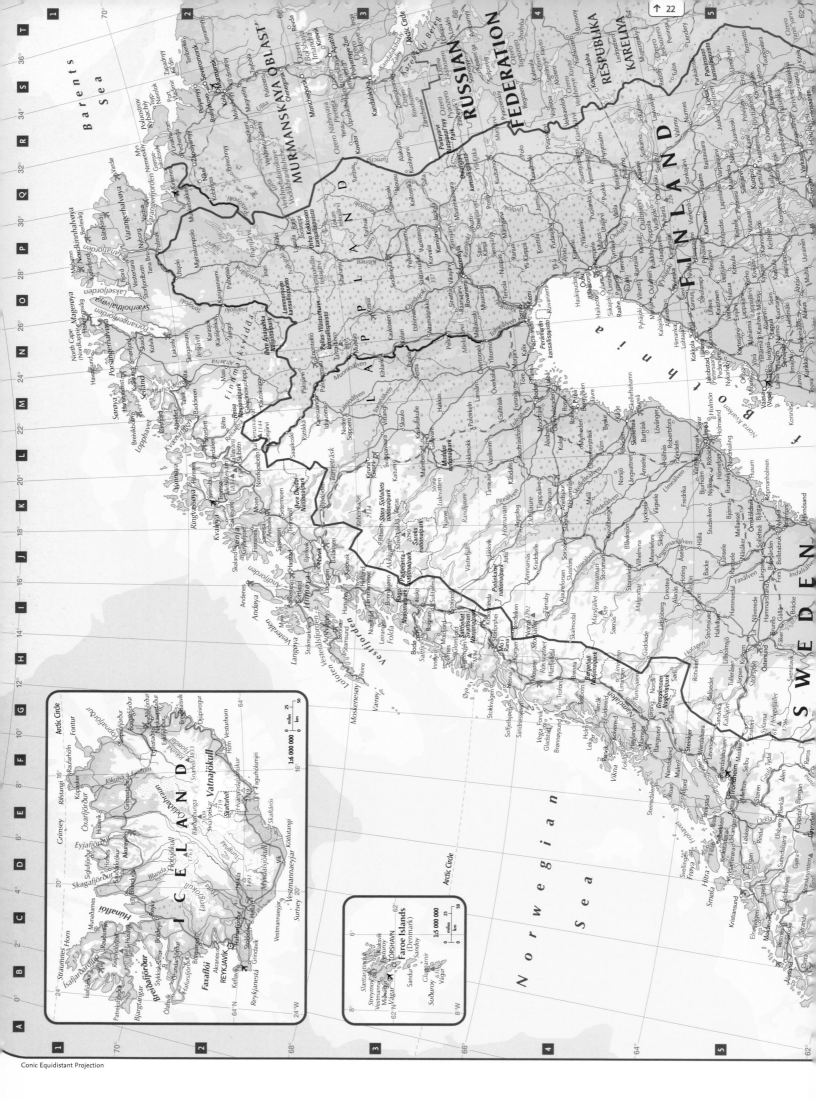

Conic Equidistant Projection

1:5 000 000

| 0 | 50 | 100 | 150 | miles |

| 0 | 50 | 100 | 150 | 200 | 250 | km |

Europe
Scandinavia and the Baltic States

Conic Equidistant Projection

12   1:5 000 000

0   50   100   150 miles
0   50   100   150   200 250 km

Europe
Northwest Europe

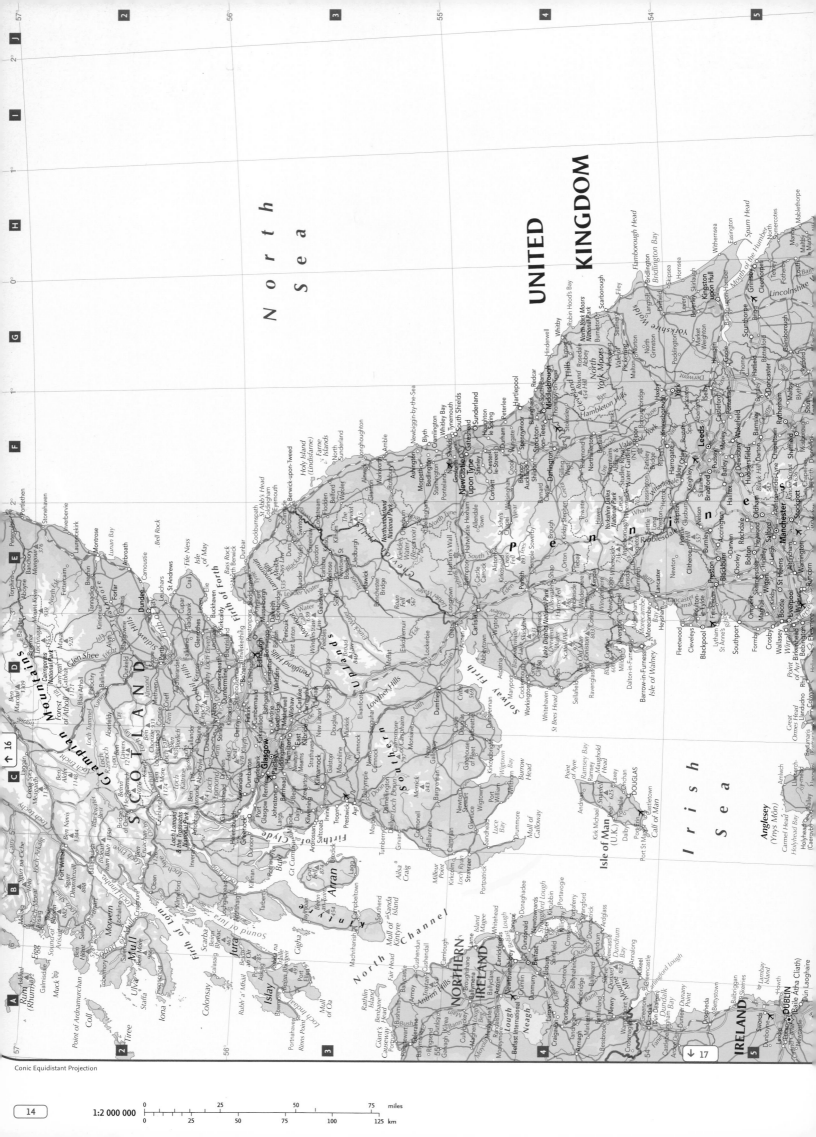

Conic Equidistant Projection

1:2 000 000

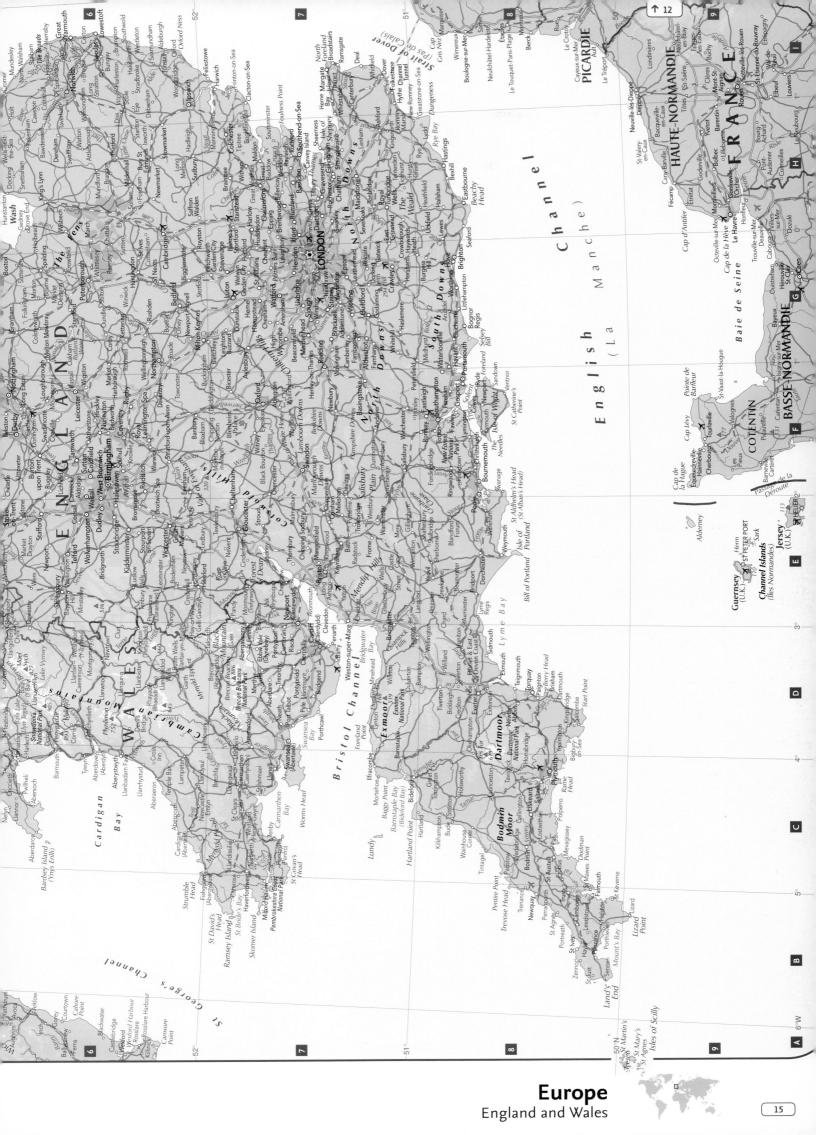

Europe
England and Wales

Europe
Scotland

1:2 000 000

Conic Equidistant Projection

16

Europe

France

Conic Equidistant Projection

1:5 000 000

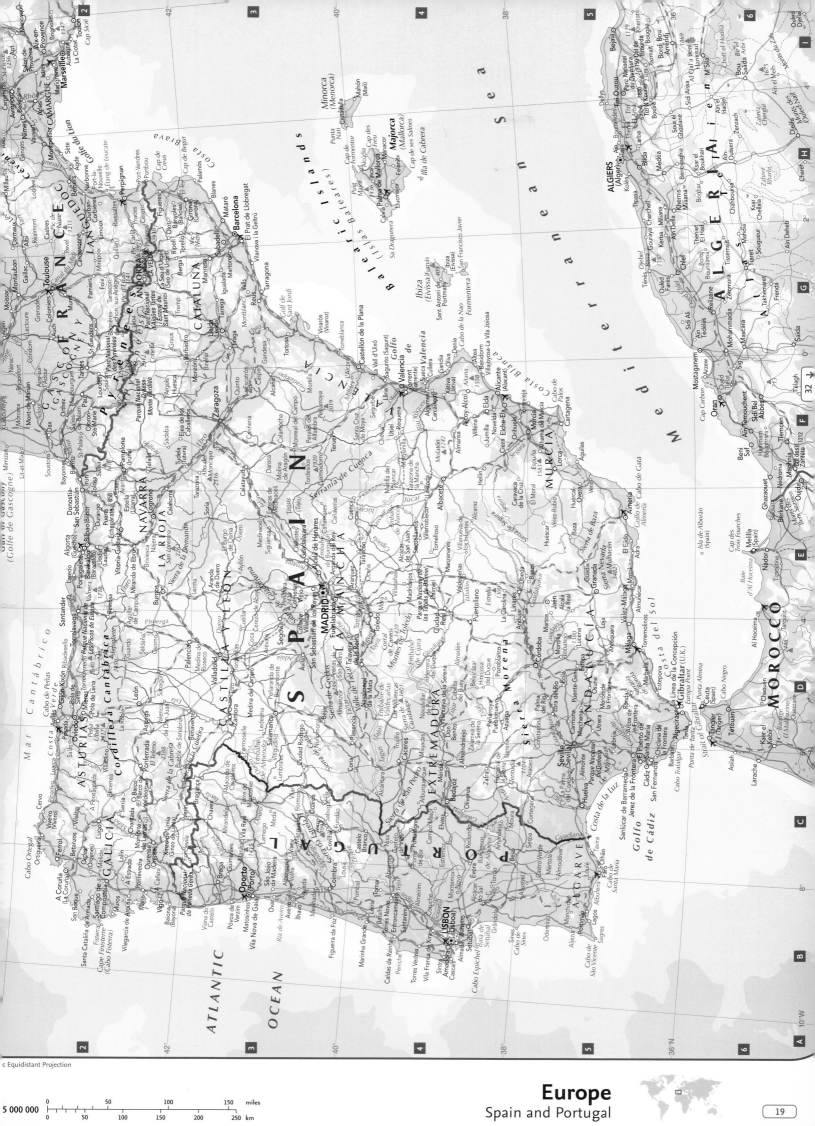

Europe
Spain and Portugal

c Equidistant Projection

5 000 000

0   50   100   150   miles
0   50   100   150   200   250 km

Conic Equidistant Projection

1:5 000 000

Europe
Western Russian Federation

OCEAN

160° 180° ① 180° 80° ② 70 ③ 60° ④ 160°

20°

T

160° S

R

OCEAN Q

P

O

N

M

L

Laptev
Sea
(More Laptevykh)

New Siberia Islands
(Novosibirskiye Ostrova)

East Siberian Sea
(Vostochno-Sibirskoye More)

Chukchi
Sea

Arctic Circle

Seward Peninsula

U.S.A.

Bering Strait

Bering
Sea

Ostrov
Bol'shoy
Lyakhovskiy

Khrebet Cherskogo

Yukagirskoye
Ploskogor'ye

Kolymskaya
Nizmennost'

Khrebet Kolymskiy

Koryakskoye Nagor'ye

Sredinnyy Khrebet

Pribilof
Islands

St Matthew
Island
(U.S.A.)

Nunivak
Island

Attu
Island
(U.S.A.)

Kiska
Island
(U.S.A.)

Aleutian Islands

170°

S I B I R (R)Y S K I Y   K h r e b e t

Verkhoyanskiy
Khrebet

Yakutsk
Pokrovsk

S I B E R I A
(SIBIR')

A
T
I
O
N

Central Siberian
Plateau

(Sredne-Sibirskoy
Ploskogor')

Sea
of
Okhotsk
(Okhotskoye More)

Magadan

Kamchatka Peninsula
(Poluostrov Kamchatka)

Petropavlovsk-
Kamchatskiy

Kuril Islands
(Kuril'skiye Ostrova)

5 160°

Bratsk

Ust'-
Ilimsk

Ust'-
Kut

Kirensk

Severo-
Baykal'skoye
Nagor'ye

Bodaybo

Stanovoy   Khrebet

Neryungri

Stanovoye
Nagor'ye

Stanovoy-Muyskiy Khrebet

Vitimskoye
Ploskogor'ye

Khrebet Dzhugdzhur

Sakhalin

Khrebet Dzhagdy

Komsomol'sk-
na-Amure

Yuzhno-Sakhalinsk

La Pérouse Strait

Hokkaido

PACIFIC

OCEAN

40°

150°

Irkutsk

Angarsk
Sibirskoye

Ulan-Ude

Khrebet Khamar-Daban

Chita
Nerchinsk

Skovorodino

Tynda

Zeya

Blagoveshchensk

Svobodnyy

Khabarovsk

Sikhote-Alin'

Sapporo

Hakodate

6

Hatgal

Mörön

ULAN BATOR
(Ulaanbaatar)

MONGOLIA

Choybalsan

Manzhouli

Hulun Buir
(Hailar)

Qiqihar

Da Hinggan Ling

MANCHURIA

Daqing (Anda)

Harbin

Hegang

Jiamusi

Jixi

Mudanjiang

Vladivostok

Nakhodka

JAPAN

TŌKYŌ
Yokohama

Sendai

Bayanhongor

Gobi   Desert

INNER MONGOLIA

Changchun

Jilin
(Kirin)

Songyuan
(Fuyu)

Tongliao

NORTH
KOREA

P'YONGYANG

Sea
of
Japan
(East Sea)

Nagoya

Osaka

Kyōto

Hiroshima

Fukuoka

Kyushu

Hohhot

Baotou

BEIJING
(Peking)
Baoding

Datong

Zhangjiakou
(Kalgan)

Shenyang

Fushun

Anshan

Benxi

Jinzhou

Chifeng
(Ulanhad)

Qinhuangdao

Dalian
(Lüda)

Tangshan

Tianjin

Bo Hai

Yantai

SEOUL
(Sŏul)

SOUTH
KOREA

Pusan

Taegu

Kwangju

Nagasaki

Yellow
Sea
(Huang Hai)

C H I N A

Wuhai
(Haibowan)

Dongying

Laiyang

7

140°

Asia

Northern Asia

25

↓ 34

Albers Conic Equal Area Projection

1:20 000 000

| 0 | | 200 | | 400 | | 600 | miles |

| 0 | 200 | 400 | 600 | 800 | 1000 km |

→ 38

G
F
E
D
C
B

6 **7** **8** **9** **10**

PACIFIC OCEAN

Northern Mariana Islands (U.S.A.)
CAPITOL HILL Saipan
Tinian
Rota

HAGÄTÑA Guam (U.S.A.)

FEDERATED STATES OF MICRONESIA

Caroline Islands
Faraulep
Sorol
Ulithi
Colonia Yap
Ngulu
Eauripik

PALAU
MELEKEOK
Palau Islands

PAPUA NEW GUINEA

New Maoke
Puncak Jaya
Central Range

Guinea

Wewak
Sepik
Balimo
Torres St.

Prince of Wales I.
Cape York Peninsula
Endeavour
Gulf of Carpentaria

QUEENSLAND
Mount Isa
Georgina

NORTHERN TERRITORY

AUSTRALIA

WESTERN AUSTRALIA

PHILIPPINES

Luzon
QUEZON CITY
MANILA
Philippine Sea
Samar
Cebu
Negros
Panay
Mindanao
Davao
General Santos
Zamboanga
Sulu Archipelago

Celebes Sea

Halmahera
Moluccas (Maluku)
Seram
Ambon
Laut Banda (Banda Sea)

Timor Sea

NORTHERN TERRITORY
Darwin
Arnhem Land
Tanami Desert

South China Sea

Paracel Islands (Xisha Qundao)

Spratly Islands

MALAYSIA

BRUNEI
BANDAR SERI BEGAWAN

Borneo

Celebes (Sulawesi)

INDONESIA

EAST TIMOR
DILI
Timor

Flores
Sumba
Lesser Sunda Islands

Ashmore and Cartier Islands (Australia)

Great Sandy Desert

VIETNAM
Ho Chi Minh City (Saigon)

THAILAND
BANGKOK

CAMBODIA
PHNOM PENH

Gulf of Thailand

LAOS

MALAYSIA
KUALA LUMPUR
PUTRAJAYA

SINGAPORE
SINGAPORE

Sumatra
Medan

Strait of Malacca

INDONESIA

JAKARTA
Bandung
Java
Surabaya
Semarang
Bali

Christmas Island (Australia)

INDIAN OCEAN

Cocos Islands (Australia)

Tropic of Capricorn

Asia
Eastern and Southeast Asia

Asia

Japan, North Korea and South Korea

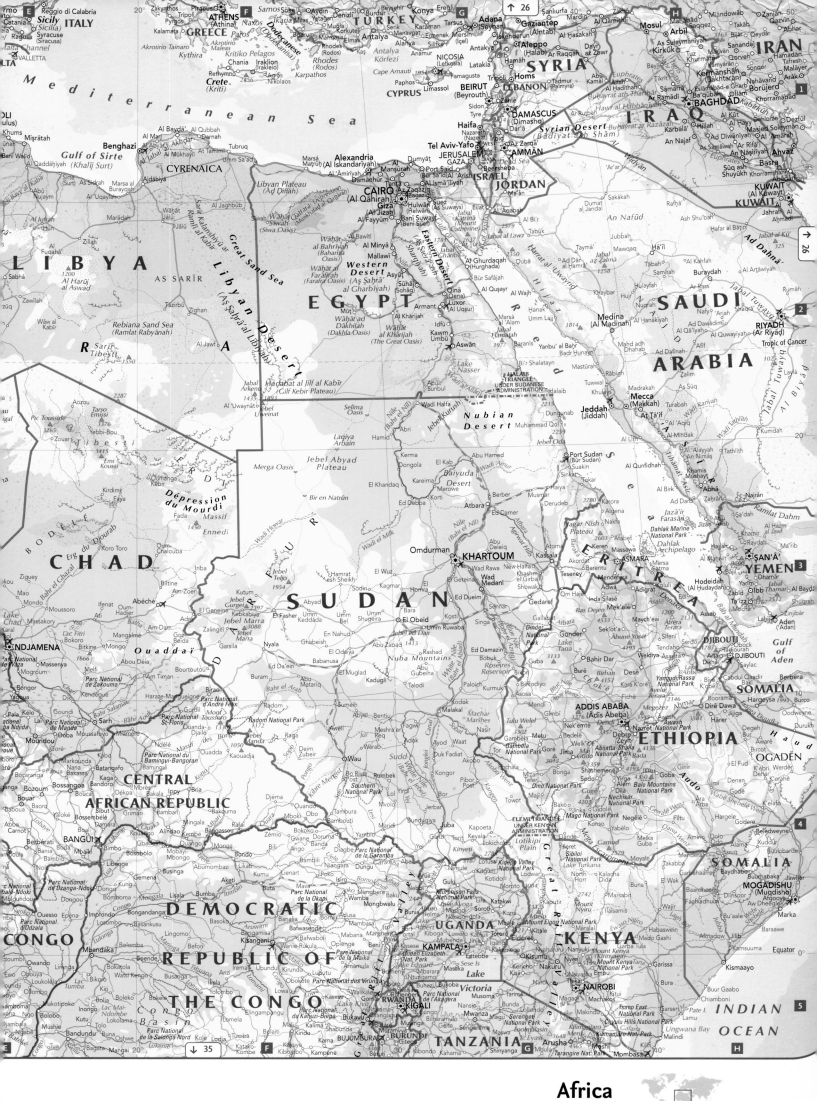

Africa

Central and Southern Africa

ATLANTIC

OCEAN

GHANZI

BOTSWANA

Central Kalahari Game Reserve

KWENE

SOUTHE

NOR

KGALAGADI

K a l a h a r i

D e s e r t

Gemsbok National Park

Matuasehube Game Reserve

Kalahari Gemsbok National Park

Kgalagadi Transfrontier Park

KHUTSE Game Reserve

Moreswe Pan

ERONGO

KHOMAS

OMAHEKE

WINDHOEK

NAMIBIA

HARDAP

N a m i b   D e s e r t

Namib-Naukluft Game Park

Tropic of Capricorn

GREAT NAMAQUALAND

KARAS

Ai-Ais Hot Springs Game Park

Ai-Ais/Richtersveld Transfrontier Park

Richtersveld National Park

Richtersveld Cultural and Botanical Landscape

NAMAQUALAND

Goegap Nature Reserve

Namaqua National Park

Augrabies Falls National Park

REPUBLI

GRIQUALAND WEST

NORTHERN

CAPE

OF

SOUTH AF

G r e a t   K a r o o

Tankwa-Karoo National Park

Karoo National Park

Camdeboo National Park

WESTERN CAPE

Table Mountain Nature Reserve

CAPE TOWN

West Coast National Park

Bontebok National Park

De Hoop Nature Reserve

Wilderness National Park

Tsitsikamma Forest and Coastal National Park

Cape of Good Hope

Lambert Azimuthal Equal Area Projection

1:5 000 000

0   50   100   150 miles

0   50 100 150 200 250 km

Africa
Republic of South Africa

INDONESIA

Borneo

Celebes
Sea

Celebes
(Sulawesi)

Equator

Laut Maluku
(Molucca Sea)

Moluccas
(Maluku)

Laut Seram
(Ceram Sea)

PAPUA

Bismarck
Archipelago

Bismarck
Sea

New
Guinea

NEW GUINEA

Laut Banda
(Banda Sea)

EAST TIMOR

EAST TIMOR

Timor

Timor
Sea

Arafura
Sea

Torres Strait

Gulf
of
Papua

PORT MORESBY

INDIAN
OCEAN

Ashmore and
Cartier Islands
(Australia)

Cape York

Cape
York
Peninsula

Gulf
of
Carpentaria

Arnhem
Land

Great Barrier Reef

Kimberley
Plateau

NORTHERN

TERRITORY

Barkly Tableland

Tanami
Desert

QUEENSLAND

Great Sandy Desert

WESTERN

AUSTRALIA

Gibson
Desert

MacDonnell
Ranges

Simpson
Desert

Great Dividing Range

Tropic of Capricorn

Hamersley Range

Great
Victoria Desert

SOUTH
AUSTRALIA

NEW SOUTH WALES

Nullarbor Plain

Great
Australian Bight

Perth

Adelaide

CANBERRA
A.C.T.

Sydney
Wollongong

VICTORIA

Melbourne

Bass Strait

TASMANIA

Hobart

40°S

Lambert Azimuthal Equal Area Projection

1:20 000 000

0   200   400   600   miles

0   200   400   600   800   1000 km

Oceania
Australia, New Zealand and Southwest Pacific

Oceania
Australia

Oceania
Southeast Australia

Lambert Azimuthal Equal Area Proj

1:5 000 000

A B C D E F

168° 170° 172° 174° 176° 178°

1
Three Kings Islands
Cape Maria van Diemen
North Cape
Te Paki
Cape Karikari
Doubtless Bay
34°
Awanui
Ahipara Bay
Tauroa Point
Kaitaia
Kerikeri
Bay of Islands
Cape Brett
Russell
Broadwood
Tangowahine
Kawakawa
Poor Knights Islands
2
Donnellys Crossing
Dargaville
Maungaturoto
Whangarei
Bream Bay
Mokohinau Islands
36°

T a s m a n

S e a

Wellsford
Leigh
North Head
Kaipara Harbour
Port Fitzroy
Little Barrier Island
Great Barrier Island
Kaiwaka
Kawau Island
Colville Channel
Warkworth
East Coast Bays
Takapuna
Hauraki Gulf
Waiheke Island
Whitianga
Mercury Islands
Coromandel Peninsula
Auckland
Manukau
Colville
Papakura
Pukekohe
Waiuku
Thames
Coromandel Range
Whangamata
Mayor Island
The Aldermen Islands
3
Manukau Harbour
Port Waikato
Huntly
Waikato
Matakana Island
Motiti Island
Whakaari 1075
Cape Runaway
Hicks Bay
Te Araroa
East Cape

N o r t h
Hamilton
Te Awamutu
Cambridge
Tauranga
Bay of Plenty
Whakatane
Opotiki
Ruatoria
Tokomaru Bay

I s l a n d
Kawhia
Kawhia Harbour
Otorohanga
Te Kuiti
Lake Rotorua
Rotorua
1117
Kawerau
Te Teko
Raukumara Range 1754
Hikurangi
4
Piopio
Tokoroa
Mangakino
Mount Tarawera
Urewera National Park
Matawai
Tolaga Bay
38°

NEW
Awakino
Mokau
Okahukura
Ohura
Taumarunui
Okatina
Lake Taupo
Tongariro National Park
Huiarau Range
Kaitawa
Gisborne
Poverty Bay
North Taranaki Bight
New Plymouth
Mount Taranaki (Mount Egmont) 2518
Egmont National Park
Whanganui National Park
Ohakune
Mount Ruapehu 2797
Kaimanawa Mountains
Tarawera
Wairoa
Nuhaka
Table Cape
Mahia Peninsula

ZEALAND
Cape Egmont
Opunake
Hawera
South Taranaki Bight
Patea
Raetihi
Waiouru
Taihape
Waipawa
Rangitikei
Bay View
Napier
Hastings
Havelock North
Cape Kidnappers
Waimarama
Hawke Bay
4
Wanganui
Turakina
Marton
Abitu
Rangitikei
Ruahine Range
Tikokino
Waipawa
Waipukurau

40°
Cape Farewell
Farewell Spit
Feilding
Palmerston North
Levin
Dannevirke
Porangahau
Cape Turnagain
Kahurangi Point
Golden Bay
Collingwood
Cape Stephens
Cape D'Urville
D'Urville Island
French Pass
Kapiti Island
Otaki
Upper Hutt
Porirua
Tararua Range
Pahiatua
Eketahuna

S o u t h

Cape Palliser
PACIFIC

OCEAN

Oceania
New Zealand

43

North America
Canada

States in the U.S.A.
numbered on the map:

1. CONNECTICUT (K5)
2. MASSACHUSETTS (K5)
3. NEW HAMPSHIRE (K5)
4. RHODE ISLAND (K5)
5. VERMONT (K5)

North America

Northeast United States

Lambert Conformal Conic Proj

1:3 500 000

50 →

Lambert Conformal Conic Projection

1 : 000 000

0   50   100   miles

0   50   100   150   200 km

Lambert Conformal Conic Projection

1:14 000 000

		miles
0	200	400
0	200 400 600	800 km

North America
Central America and the Caribbean

A T L A N T I C

O C E A N

Equator

GEORGETOWN
New Amsterdam
Linden
Nieuw
Nickerie Onverwacht
Apoera
PARAMARIBO
Brokopondo
Professor van
Blommestein Meer
SURINAME
Wilhelmina
Ceberge
Juliana Top
French
Guiana
CAYENNE
Pointe Isère
Organabo
St-Laurent-
du-Maroni
Albina
Kourou
Pointe Béhague
Régina
Cabo Orange
Oyapock
Cabo Cassiporé
Parque Nacional
de Cabo Orange
Ilha de Maracá
Calçoene
Amapá
BRAZIL

Mouths of the
Amazon

Macapá
Afuá
Ilha Caviana
Ilha Mexiana
Baía de Marajó
Salinópolis
Soure
Ilha
de Marajó
Vigia
Bragança
Belém
Castanhal
Capanema
Viseu

São Luís
Parque Nacional dos
Lençóis Maranhenses
Fortaleza
(Ceará)

Natal

João Pessoa

Recife
(Pernambuco)

Maceió

Salvador
(Bahia)

BRASÍLIA

Goiânia

Belo
Horizonte

Vitória

Campo
Grande

São Paulo

Rio de
Janeiro

South America
Northern South America

South America
Southern South America

Lambert Azimuthal Equal Area Proje

1:14 000 000

South America
Southeast Brazil

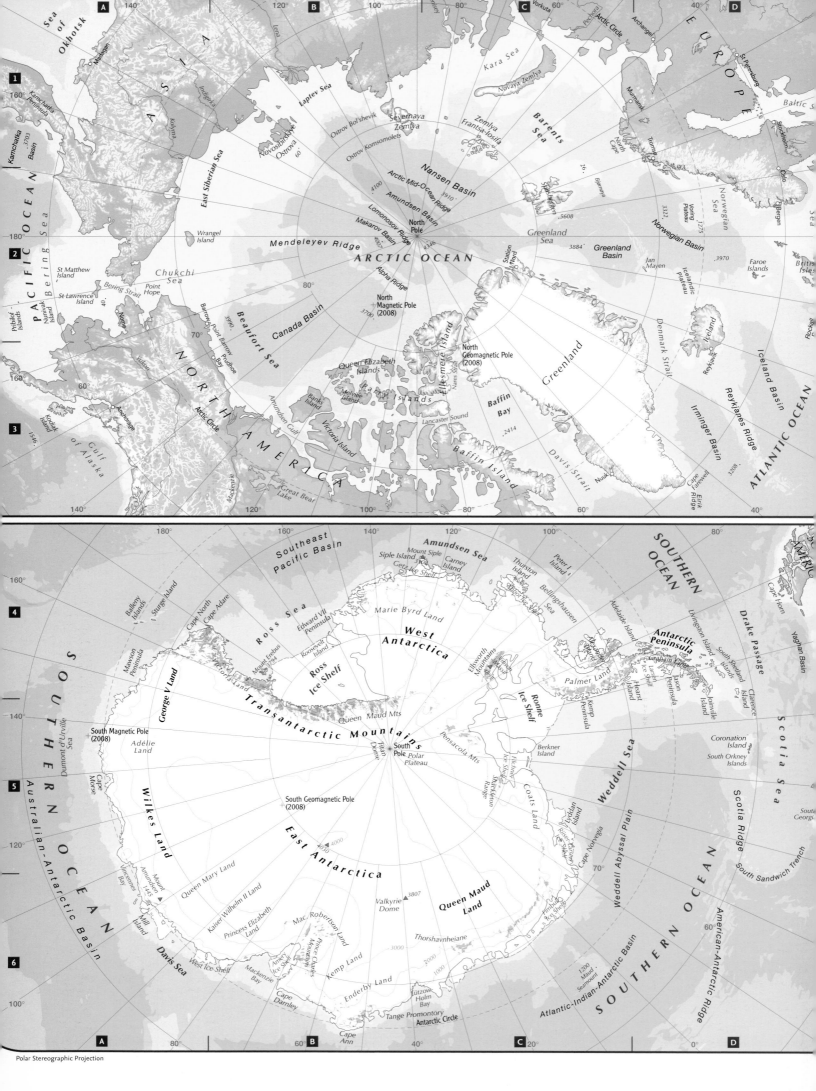

Arctic Ocean and Antarctica

Polar Stereographic Projection

1:35 000 000

Index

The index includes the most significant names on the maps in the atlas. The names are generally indexed to the largest scale map on which they appear. For large physical features this will be the largest scale map on which they appear in their entirety or in the majority. Names can be located using the grid reference letters and numbers around the edges of the map. Names located on insets have a symbol □.

Abbreviations used to describe features in the index:

admin. dist.	administrative district	g.	gulf	pt	point
admin. div.	administrative division	hd.	headland	prov.	province
admin. reg.	administrative region	i.	island	r.	river
aut. reg.	autonomous region	imp. lake	impermanent lake	r. mouth	river mouth
aut. rep.	autonomous republic	is	islands	reg.	region
b.	bay	l.	lake	resr	reservoir
c.	cape	lag.	lagoon	salt l.	salt lake
depr.	depression	mt.	mountain	sea chan.	sea channel
des.	desert	mts	mountains	terr.	territory
esc.	escarpment	pen.	peninsula	vol.	volcano
est.	estuary	plat.	plateau		
for.	forest	pref.	prefecture		

58

Dapitan 29E7
Da Qaidam Zhen 27I3
Daqing 30B3
Dara 32B3
Da'ī 33G1
Darazo 32B3
Dardanelles *strait* 21L4
Dar es Salaam 35D4
Dargaville 43D2
Darīan 27J2
Darién, Golfo del g. 52C2
Darjiling 27H4
Darling r. 42B3
Darling Downs *hills* 42D1
Darlington 14F4
Darmstadt 13L6
Darnah 33F1
Daroca 19F3
Darovskoy 22J4
Dartford 15H7
Dartmoor *hills* 15C8
Dartmouth 15D8
Dartmouth 45L5
Daru 38E2
Darwen 14E5
Darwin 40E2
Daşkäsän 23J8
Daşoguz 26E2
Datça 21L6
Date 30F4
Datong 27K2
Daugava r. 11N8
Daugavpils 11O9
Davao 29E7
Davenport 47I3
Daventry 15F6
Daveyton 37I4
Davis 49H1
David 51H7
Davis Strait *strait* 45M3
Dawqah 26E5
Dawson Creek 44F4
Dax 18D5
Daylesford 42B6
Dayr az Zawr 33H1
Dayton 47K4
Daytona Beach 47K6
Dazhou 27J3
Dead Sea *salt l.* 33G1
Deal 15I7
Dean, Forest of 15E7
Deán Funes 54D4
Dearne r. 14F5
Death Valley *depr.* 49D2
Deauville 15H9
Debar 21I4
Debrecen 21I1
Debre Zeyit 34D3
Decatur 47J5
Decatur 47J5
Deccan *plat.* 27G5
Deception Bay 42F1
Děčín 13O5
Decorah 47I3
Dédougou 32C3
Dedovichi 22F4
Dee *r.* 14D5
Dee *r. est.* 14D5
Dee *r.* 16G3
Degema 32D4
Deggendorf 13N6
Dehloran 33H1
Dej 21J1
De Kalb 47J3
Dékoa 34B3
Delap-Uliga-Djarrit 7
Delareyville 37G4
Delaware r. 48D3
Delaware *state* 48D3
Delémont 18H3
Delft 12J4
Delfzijl 13K4
Delhi 27G4
Dellys 19F5
Del Mar 49D4
Delmenhorst 13L4
Delnice 20F2
De-Longa, Ostrova *is* 25Q2
Del Río 46G6
Delsbo 11J6
Delta 46F4
Demba 35C4
Demidov 23F5
Deming 46F5
Demirci 21M5
Demirköy 21L4
Denakil *reg.* 33H3
Denbigh 14D5
Dengkou 27J2
Den Helder 12J4
Denia 19C4
Denison 47I3
Denizli 21M6
Denman 42E4
Denmark *country* 11F8
Denmark Strait *strait* 45P3
Denny 16F4
Denpasar 29D8
Denton 47I5
D'Entrecasteaux, Point 40E6
D'Entrecasteaux Islands 41K1
Denver 46F4
Denver 48C2
Deputatskiy 25O3
Dera Ghazi Khan 27G3
Derby 15F6
Derby 48E2
Dereham 15H6
Derg, Lough l. 17D5
Dergachi 23K6
Derhachi 23H6
De Ridder 47I5
Derry 17D3
De Rust 36F7
Derwent r. 14F4
Derwent r. 14G5
Derzhavinsk 26F1
Desē 34D3
Des Moines 47I3
Desna r. 23F6
Desnogorsk 23G5
Dessau 13L5
Dete 35C5
Detmold 13L5
Detroit 47K3
Detroit Lakes 47H2
Deutschlandsberg 13O7
Deva 21J2
Deventer 13K4
Devil's Lake 46H2
Devizes 15F7
Devnya 21L4
Devon Island 45I2
Devonport 41J8
Devrek 21N4
Dewas 27G4
Dewsbury 14F5
Deyang 27J3
Dezfūl 33H1
Dezhneva, Mys c. 25T3
Dhaka 27H4
Dhahran 34F1
Dhamār 34E2
Dhanbad 27H4

Dhar Adrar *hills* 32B3
Ďhar Oualâta *hills* 32C3
Dhar Tîchît *hills* 32C3
Ďharwad 27G4
Dhule 27G4
Dhuusa Marreeb 34E3
Diablo, Mount 49B2
Diablo Range *mts* 49B2
Diamante 54D4
Diamantina 55C2
Diamantina, Chapada *plat.* 55C1
Diamantina 53G6
Dianópolis 53I6
Diapaga 32D3
Dibaya 35C4
Dibrugarh 27I4
Dickinson 46G2
Didiéni 32C3
Diébougou 32C3
Diéma 32C3
Dieppe 15I9
Dietikon 18I3
Diffa 32E3
Digne-les-Bains 18H4
Dijon 18G3
Dikhil 34E2
Dikili 21L5
Dikson 24J2
Dīla 34D3
Dili 29E8
Dillingham 44C4
Dillon 46E2
Dilolo 35C5
Dimapur 27I4
Dimitrovgrad 22K5
Dimitrovgrad 23K5
Dinan 18C2
Dinant 12J5
Dinar 21N5
Dinaric Alps *mts* 20G2
Dindigul 27G5
Dingle Bay 17B5
Dinguiraye 32B3
Dingwall 16E3
Dioila 32C3
Dionisio Cerqueira 54F3
Diourbel 32B3
Dipayal 27H4
Diré 32C3
Dirē Dawa 34E3
Dirk Hartog Island 40C5
Dirs 34E2
Discovery Bay 41I7
Distrito Federal *admin. dist.* 55B1
Ditloung 36F3
Divinópolis 55B3
Divnoye 23I7
Divo 32C4
Dixon 49B1
Dixon Entrance *sea chan.* 44E4
Diyarbakır 26E4
Djado, Plateau du 32E2
Djambala 34B4
Djelfa 19H6
Djenné 32C3
Djibo 32C3
Djibouti 34E2
Djibouti *country* 34E2
Djougou 32D4
Djoum 32E4
Dmitriyev-L'govskiy 23G5
Dmitrov 22H4
Dnieper r. 23F6
Dniester r. 23F6
Dniester r. 23F7
Dniprodzerzhyns'k 23G6
Dnipropetrovs'k 23G6
Dno 22F4
Doba 33E4
Dobele 11M8
Doberai, Jazirah *pen.* 29F8
Doboj 20H2
Dobrich 21L3
Dobrinka 23I5
Dobrush 23F5
Dodge City 46G4
Dodoma 35D4
Dogondoutchi 32D3
Doğu Menteşe Dağları *mts* 21M6
Doha 34F1
Dokkum 13J4
Dokshytsy 11I9
Dokuchayevs'k 23H7
Dole 18G3
Dolgellau 15D6
Dolgorukovo 23H5
Dolisie 34B4
Dolomites *mts* 20D2
Dolores 54E5
Dolores 54E5
Dolyna 23I6
Domažlice 13N6
Dombóvár 20H1
Domeyko 54B3
Dominica *country* 51L5
Dominican Republic *country* 51J5
Domokos 21J5
Dompu 29D8
Don r. 16G3
Don r. 23I7
Donaghadee 17G3
Donald 42A6
Don Benito 19D4
Doncaster 14F5
Dondo 35A4
Donegal 17D3
Donegal Bay 17D3
Donets r. 23H7
Donets'kyy Kryazh *hills* 23H6
Dongchuan 27J4
Dongfang 28J5
Dongguan 31B5
Đông Hới 29C6
Dongning 30D3
Dongola 33G3
Dongting Hu l. 27K4
Dongying 27K3
Donostia-San Sebastián 19F5
Donskoye 23I7
Doomadgee 41H3
Dorchester 15E8
Dordogne r. 18D4
Dordrecht 12J5
Dores do Indaiá 55B2
Dori 32C3
Dorking 15G7
Dornoch Firth *est.* 16E3
Doro 32C3
Dorogobuzh 23G5
Dorohoi 21J1
Dorrigo 42F3
Dosso 32D3
Dothan 47J5

Douala 32D4
Douentza 32C3
Douglas 46F3
Douglas 46F5
Douglas 47J5
Dourados 54F2
Douro r. 19B3
Dover 15I7
Dover 48A2
Dover 48D2
Dover 48F1
Dover, Strait of *strait* 15I8
Dover r. 15D6
Downpatrick 17G3
Doylestown 48D2
Drāa, Hamada du *plat.* 32C2
Dracena 55A3
Drachten 13K4
Drăgănești-Olt 21K2
Drăgășani 21K2
Draguignan *mts* 37I3
Drakensberg *mts* 37I3
Drammen 11G7
Drava r. 20H2
Dréan 20B6
Dresden 13N5
Dreux 18E2
Drobeta-Turnu Severin 21J2
Drogheda 17F4
Drohobych 23D6
Droitwich Spa 15E6
Dromore 17E3
Dronfield 14F5
Drummondville 45K5
Druskininkai 11N10
Druzhnaya Gorka 11Q7
Dryanovo 21K3
Duartina 55A3
Dubai 26E4
Dubawnt Lake 45H3
Dubbo 42D4
Dublin 17F4
Dublin 47K5
Dubno 23E6
Dubovka 23I6
Dubovskoye 23I7
Dubrovnik 20H3
Dubrovytsya 23E6
Dubuque 47I3
Dudinka 24J3
Dudley 15E6
Duékoué 32C4
Duero r. 19E3
Dufourspitze *mt.* 18H4
Dugi Rat 20G3
Duisburg 13K5
Dukathole 37H6
Dukhovnitskoye 23K5
Dulovo 21L3
Duluth 47I2
Dumaguete 29E7
Dumai 27J5
Dumas 46G4
Dumbarton 16E5
Dumfries 16F5
Dumyāt 33G1
Dunajská Streda 13P7
Dunakeszi 21H1
Dunaújváros 20H1
Dunavtsi 23E6
Duncan 46H5
Duncansby Head 16F2
Dundaga 11M8
Dundalk 17F3
Dundalk 48C3
Dundalk Bay 17F4
Dundas 48B1
Dundee 16G4
Dundee 37J5
Dundonald 17G3
Dunedin 43C7
Dunfermline 16F4
Dungannon 17F3
Dungarvan 17E5
Dungeness *hd* 15H8
Dungiven 17F3
Dungog 42E4
Dungun 29C7
Dunhua 30C4
Dunkerque 18F1
Dunkirk 48B1
Dún Laoghaire 17F4
Dunmore 48D1
Dunmurry 17G3
Dunnet Head 16F2
Dunnville 48B1
Duns 16G5
Dunstable 15G7
Durağan 23G8
Durango 19E2
Durango 46F4
Durango 46G7
Durant 47I5
Durazno 54E4
Durban 37J5
Durban-Corbières 18F5
Durbanville 36D7
Durham 14F4
Durham 47L4
Durlești 21M1
Durrës 21H4
Durrington 15F7
Dursunbey 21M5
Dushanbe 27F3
Düsseldorf 13K5
Dutse 32D3
Dutsin-Ma 32D3
Duyun 27J4
Düzce 21N4
Dwarka 27F4
Dyat'kovo 23G5
Dyersburg 47J4
Dymytrov 23G6
Dzaoudzi 35E5
Dzerzhinsk 22I4
Dzhankoy 23G7
Dzhusaly 26J7
Działdowo 13R4
Dziuahnmod 27J2
Dzyarzhynsk 11O10

East Orange 48D2
East Providence 48F2
East Siberian Sea 25P2
East Timor *country* 29E8
East York 48B1
Eau Claire 47I3
Ebbw Vale 15D7
Ebebiyin 32E4
Eberswalde-Finow 13N4
Ebetsu 30F4
Eboli 20F4
Ebolowa 32E4
Ebro r. 19G3
Écija 19D5
Eckernförde 13L3
Ecuador *country* 52C4
Ed 33H3
Eday i. 16G1
Ed Damazin 33G3
Ed Damer 33G3
Ed Dueim 33G3
Edéa 32E4
Edéia 55A2
Eden 47J5
Edenderry 17E4
Edessa 21J4
Edinburg 46H6
Edinburgh 16F5
Edirne 21L4
Edmonton 44G4
Edmundston 45L5
Edremit 21L5
Edward, Lake 34C4
Edwards Plateau 46G6
Effingham 47J4
Eger 13R7
Egersund 11E7
Egilsstaðir 10□ 2
Egirdir 21N6
Egmont, Cape 43D4
Egvekinot 25T3
Egypt *country* 33G2
Ehen Hudag 27J3
Ehingen (Donau) 13L6
Eiel *mts* 13K5
Eigg i. 16C4
Eighty Mile Beach 40E3
Eilat 33G2
Eindhoven 12J5
Einsiedeln 18I3
Eirunepé 52E5
Eisenach 13M5
Eisenhüttenstadt 13O4
Eisenstadt 13P7
Ekenäs 11H7
Ekibastuz 27G1
Eksjö 11I8
El Aouinet 20B7
El Arrouch 20B6
Elazığ 26C3
Elba, Isola d' i. 20D3
El'ban 30E2
Elbasan 21I4
Elbe r. 13L4
Elbert, Mount 46F4
Elbeuf 17I2
Elbląg 13Q3
Elbrus *mt.* 23I8
Elburz Mountains *mts* 26D3
El Cajon 49D4
El Callao 52F2
El Campo 47H6
El Centro 49E4
El Cerro 52F7
Elche-Elx 19F4
Elda 19F4
El'dikan 25O3
El Dorado 47H4
El Dorado 47I5
Eldorado 54F3
Eldoret 34D3
El Ejido 19E5
Elemi Triangle *terr.* 34D3
Eleuthera i. 47L6
El Fasher 33F3
El Fuerte 46F4
El Geneina 33F3
Elgin 16F3
Elgin 47J3
El Golea 32D1
Elgon, Mount 26C6
El Hadjar 20B6
El Hank *esc.* 32C2
Elías Piña 51J5
Elista 23J7
Elizabeth 48D2
Elizabeth City 47L4
Elizabethtown 47J4
El Jadida 32C1
El Jem 20D7
Efk 13Q4
El Kala 20C6
Elk City 46H4
El Kelaâ des Srarhna 32C1
Elkford 46F1
Elk Grove 49B1
Elkhart 47J3
Elkhovo 21L3
Elkins 48B3
Elko 46D3
Elkton 48D3
Ellensburg 46C2
Ellesmere Island 45J2
Ellesmere Port 14E5
Ellicott City 48C3
Elliot 37H6
El Golea 32D1
Ellsworth 47N3
Elmalı 21M6
El Meghaïer 32D1
Elmira 48C1
Elmshorn 13L4
El Muglad 33F3
El Obeid 33G3
El Oued 32D1
El Paso 46F5
El Porvenir 46G4
El Porvenir 51J7
El Prat de Llobregat 19H3
El Progreso 50G5
El Puerto de Santa María 19C5
El Reno 46H4
El Salto 46F7
El Salvador *country* 50G6
Elsinore 49D4
El Tarf 20C6
El Tigre 52F2
El'ton 23J6
Elvas 19C4
Elverum 11G6
Ely 15H6
Elyria 47K3
Emba 26J2
Embalenhle 37I4
Embarcación 54D2
Embu 34D4
Emden 13K4
Emet 21M5
Emi Koussi *mt.* 33E3
Emirdağ 21N5
Mjiindini 37J3
Emmaboda 11I8
Emmaus 48D2

eMzinoni 37I4
Encarnación 54E3
Encinitas 49D5
Encruzilhada 55C1
Endeavour Strait 41I2
Endicott 48C1
Enerhodar 23G7
Enez r. 19G3
England *admin. div.* 15E6
English Channel *strait* 15F9
Enid 46H4
Eniwa 30F4
Enköping 11J7
Enna 20F6
Ennis 17D5
Ennis 47H5
Enniscorthy 17E5
Enniskillen 17E3
Enschede 13K4
Ensenada 46D5
Enshi 27J3
Entebbe 34D3
Entre Rios de Minas 55B3
Entroncamento 19B4
Enugu 32D4
Envira 52D5
Ephrata 48C2
Épinal 18H2
Epsom 15G7
Equatorial Guinea *country* 32D4
Érd 20H1
Erdek 21L4
Erechim 54F3
Ereğli 21N4
Ereğli 33G1
Erenhot 27K2
Erfurt 13M5
'Erg Chech *des.* 32C2
Ergli 11N8
Erie 48A1
Erie, Lake 48J1
Eritrea *country* 34D2
Erlangen 13M6
Ermelo 37I4
Ermenek 33G1
Ermoupoli 21K6
Erode 27G5
Erongo *admin. reg.* 36B1
Er Rachidia 32C1
Ertil' 23I6
Erzgebirge *mts* 13N5
Erzincan 26C3
Erzurum 26D3
Esbjerg 11F9
Escanaba 47J2
Escárcega 50F5
Eschwege 13M5
Escondido 49D4
Escuinapa 50D4
Escuintla 50F6
Eséka 32E4
Eşfahān 26E3
Esik 27H2
Esikhawini 37K5
Esikisitura 11J7
Eskişehir 21J8
Eskişehir 21N5
Eslāmābād-e Gharb 33H1
Eslöv 11H9
Eşme 21M5
Esmeraldas 52C3
Esperance 40E6
Esperanza 54D3
Espinhaço, Serra do *mts* 55C2
Espinosa 55C1
Espírito Santo *state* 55C2
Espíritu Santo i. 39G3
Espoo 11N6
Esquel 54B6
Es Semara 32B2
Essaouira 32C1
Essen 13K5
Essequibo r. 53G2
Essex 48C3
Esstocourt 37H5
Estância 53K6
Estella 19F5
Estepona 19D5
Estevan 46G2
Estherville 47I3
Estonia *country* 11N7
Estrela 55A5
Estrela, Serra da *mts* 19C3
Estrela do Sul 55B2
Estremoz 19C4
Etampes 18F2
Etawah 27H4
Ethandakukhanya 37J4
Ethiopia *country* 34D3
Etna, Mount *vol.* 20F6
Etobicoke 48B1
Etosha Pan *salt pan* 35B5
Euclid 48C2
Euclides da Cunha 53K6
Eugene 46C3
Euphrates r. 26D3
Euphrates r. 33H1
Eura 11M6
Eureka 46C3
Eureka 46D2
Euroa 42B6
Europa, Île i. 35E6
Europa Point 19D5
Evans City 48A2
Evanston 46E3
Evansville 47J4
Evaton 37I4
Everard Range *hills* 40G5
Everest, Mount 27H4
Everett 46C2
Everglades *swamp* 47K6
Evesham 15F6
Évora 19C4
Évreux 18E2
Evvoia i. 21K5
Ewe, Loch b. 16D3
Ewo 34B4
Exe r. 15D8
Exeter 15D8
Exeter 48F1
Exmoor *hills* 15D7
Exmouth 40A4
Exmouth 15D8
Exmouth Gulf 40C4
Exton 48D2
Extremadura *aut. comm.* 19D4
Eyasi, Lake *salt l.* 34D4
Eyemouth 16G5
Eyjafjörður *inlet* 10□ 2
Eynsham 15F7
Eyre (North), Lake *salt flat* 41H5
Eyre (South), Lake *salt flat* 41H5
Eyre Peninsula 41H6

Florin 49B1
Florina 21I4
Florø 11D6
Foça 21L5
Focșani 21K2
Foggia 20F4
Foix 18E5
Folda *sea chan.* 10I3
Foligno 20E3
Folkestone 15I7
Follonica 20D3
Fomboni 35E5
Fond du Lac 47J3
Fondi 20E4
Fonte Boa 52E4
Fontur *pt* 10□ 2
Foraker, Mount 44C3
Forchheim 13M6
Fordham 15H6
Fordingbridge 15F7
Forécariah 32B4
Forest 47J5
Forest Hill 42C5
Forestville 49A1
Forfar 16G4
Forio 20E4
Forli 20E2
Formby 14D5
Formiga 55B3
Formosa 54E3
Formosa 55B1
Formoso r. 55A1
Forrest City 47I4
Forssa 11M6
Forster 42F4
Fortaleza 53K4
Fort-de-France 51L6
Fort Dodge 47I3
Fort Edward 48E1
Forth r. 16F4
Forth, Firth of *est.* 16F4
Fort Frances 47I2
Fort Lauderdale 47K6
Fort Macleod 46E2
Fort McMurray 44G4
Fort Myers 47K6
Fort Peck 46F2
Fort Pierce 47K6
Fort Portal 34D3
Fort Scott 47I4
Fort Smith 44G3
Fort Smith 47I4
Fort Stockton 46G5
Fort Wayne 47J3
Fort William 16D4
Fort Worth 47H5
Fossano 20B2
Foster 42C7
Fougères 18D2
Fouman 23I8
Foula i. 16□
Foumban 32E4
Foveaux Strait 43A8
Fowler 46G4
Fox Creek 44G4
Foxe Basin g. 45K3
Foyle r. 17E3
Foyle, Lough b. 17E2
Foz do Iguaçu 54F3
Framingham 48F1
Franca 55B3
Francavilla Fontana 20G4
France *country* 18F3
Franceville 34B4
Francistown 35C6
Frankfort 47K4
Frankfurt am Main 13L5
Frankfurt an der Oder 13O4
Fränkische Alb *hills* 13M6
Frankland 42B2
Franklin 48B2
Franklin 47I5
Franklin D. Roosevelt Lake *resr* 46D2
Fransta 42B7
Frantsa-Iosifa, Zemlya *is* 24G2
Frascati 20E4
Fraser r. 44F5
Fraser r. 45L4
Fraser *country* 18F3
Frauenfeld 18I3
Fray Bentos 54E4
Frechen 48G4
Freckleton 14E5
Frederick 13L9
Frederick 48C3
Fredericksburg 46H5
Fredericksburg 48C3
Fredericton 45L5
Frederikshavn 11H9
Frederiksværk 11H9
Fredonia 48B1
Fredrikstad 11G7
Freehold 48D2
Freeport 47J6
Freeport City 47L6
Freetown 32B4
Free State *prov.* 37H5
Freiberg 13N5
Freiburg im Breisgau 13K6
Freising 13M6
Freistadt 13O6
Fréjus 18H5
Fremantle 40D6
Fremont 47I3
Fremont 49B2
French Guiana *terr.* 53H3
French Polynesia *terr.* 6
French Southern and Antarctic Lands *terr.* 7
Frenda 19G6
Fresnillo 50D4
Fresno 49C3
Freudenstadt 13L6
Fria 32B3
Frias 54C3
Fribourg 18H3
Friedrichshafen 13L7
Frobisher Bay 45L3
Frohavet b. 10F5
Frolovo 23I6
Frome 15E7
Frome, Lake *salt flat* 41H6
Frontera 50F5
Fronteras 46F5
Front Royal 48B3
Frosinone 20E4
Frýdek-Místek 13Q6
Fuenlabrada 19D4
Fuerte Olimpo 54E2
Fuerteventura i. 32B2
Fujairah 26E4
Fuji 31C6
Fujin 30C3
Fujinomiya 31E6
Fujiyoshida 31D6
Fukui 31E5
Fukuoka 31C6
Fukushima 31F5
Fulda 13L5
Fullerton 49D4
Fulton 48C1
Funabashi 31E6
Funafuti *atoll* 39H2
Funchal 32B1
Fundão 55C2
Fundy, Bay of g. 45L5

Gaalkacyo 34E3
Gabela 35B5
Gabès 32E1
Gabès, Golfe de g. 32E1
Gabon *country* 34B4
Gaborone 37G3
Gabrovo 21K3
Gabú 32B3
Găești 21K2
Gafsa 20C7
Gagarin 23G5
Gagnoa 32C4
Gagra 23I8
Gainesville 47I5
Gainesville 47I6
Gainesville 47K6
Gainsborough 14G5
Gairdner, Lake *salt flat* 41H6
Galana r. 35D4
Galapagos Islands 52□
Galashiels 16G5
Galați 21L2
Galatina 20H4
Galcaio 21M5
Galesburg 47I3
Galeshewe 36G5
Galich 22I4
Galicia *aut. comm.* 19C2
Gallatin 47J4
Galle 27J6
Gallinas, Punta *pt* 52D1
Gallipoli 20H4
Gallipoli 21L4
Gällivare 10L3
Gallup 46F4
Galtee Mountains *hills* 17D5
Galveston 47J6
Galveston Bay 47J6
Galway 17C4
Galway Bay 17C4
Gamalakhe 37J6
Gambēla 34D3
Gamboma 34B4
Gamleby 11J8
Gäncä 23J8
Ganda 35B5
Gandajika 35C4
Gander 45M5
Gandhinagar 27G4
Gandía 19F4
Ganganagar 27G4
Ganges r. 27I4
Ganges, Mouths of the 27H4
Gannan 30A3
Gannett Peak 44H5
Ganye 32E4
Gaoua 32C3
Gaoual 32C3
Gap 18H4
Garabogazköl Aylagy b. 26E2
Garalo 32C3
Garanhuns 53K5
Ga-Rankuwa 37I3
Garbaharrey 34E3
Garda, Lake 20D2
Garden City 46G4
Gardez 27F3
Gargždai 11L9
Garies 36C6
Garissa 34D4
Garoowe 34E3
Garopaba 55A5
Garoua 32E4
Garry r. 47J3
Garza García 46G6
Gascony, Gulf of 18C5
Gascoyne r. 40C5
Gashua 32E3
Gasparillo 51M6
Gaspé 45L5
Gaspésie, Péninsule de la *pen.* 47N2
Gastonia 47K4
Gatchina 11Q7
Gateshead 14F4
Gatesville 46H5
Gauteng *prov.* 37I4
Gävle 11J6
Gavdos i. 21J7
Gawler 41H6
Gawler Ranges *hills* 41H6
Gaya 32D3
Gaya 27H4
Gaydén 41K5
Gaylord 47K2
Gaza 23C5
Gaza *prov.* 37J2
Gaziantep 33G1
Gazimağusa 23H9
Gdańsk 13Q3
Gdańsk, Gulf of 13Q3
Gdynia 13Q3
Gedaref 33G3
Geelong 42B7
Gejiu 27J4
Gela 20F6
Gelendzhik 23H7
Gemena 34B3
Gemlik 21N4
Gemona del Friuli 20E1
General Acha 54D5
General Alvear 54C5
General Juan Madariaga 54E5
General Pico 54D5
General Roca 54C5
General Salgado 55A3
General Santos 29E7
General Villegas 54D5
Geneva 18H3
Geneva 48C1
Geneva, Lake 18H3
Genhe 30A2
Genil r. 19E5
Genk 13J5

Genoa 20C2
Genoa, Gulf of 20C2
Geographe Bay 40D6
Geographe Channel 40C4
George 36F7
George Town 29C7
Georgetown 32B3
Georgetown 46H5
Georgetown 47L5
George Town 51H5
Georgetown 53G2
Georgia *country* 23I8
Georgia *state* 47K5
Georgian Bay 45J5
Georgiyevka 27J2
Georgiyevsk 23I7
Gera 13N5
Geral de Goiás, Serra *hills* 55B1
Geral do Paraná, Serra *hills* 55B1
Geraldton 40C5
Gerede 23G8
Germany *country* 13L5
Gerze 23H8
Gettysburg 48C3
Gevgelija 21J4
Geyve 21N4
Ghadāmis 32D1
Ghana *country* 32C4
Ghanzi 35C6
Ghanzi *admin. dist.* 36F2
Ghardaïa 32D1
Gharyān 33E1
Ghazal, Bahr el *watercourse* 33E3
Ghazaouet 19F6
Ghaziabad 27G4
Ghazni 26F3
Ghent 12J5
Gheorgheni 21K1
Gherla 21J1
Ghisonaccia 18I5
Giaginskaya 23I7
Giannitsa 21J4
Giant's Causeway *lava field* 17F2
Giarre 20F6
Gibraltar 19D5
Gibraltar, Strait of *strait* 19C6
Gibson Desert 40E4
Gießen 13L5
Gifu 31E6
Gijón-Xixón 19D2
Gila r. 49F5
Gila Bend 49F5
Gilbués 53I5
Gilgandra 42D3
Gilgit 27G3
Gillette 46F3
Gillingham 15H7
Gilroy 49B2
Ginosa 20G4
Gioia del Colle 20F4
Gippsland reg. 42B7
Giresun 23H8
Girona 19H3
Girvan 16E5
Gisborne 43G4
Gislaved 11H8
Gisors 18F2
Gitarama 34C4
Gitega 34C4
Giulianova 20E3
Giurgiu 21K3
Giyani 37J2
Giza 33G2
Gjakovë 21I3
Gjilan 21I3
Gjirokastër 21I4
Gjøvik 11G6
Glace Bay 45M5
Gladstone 41K4
Gladstone 42A4
Glamoč 20G2
Glasgow 16E5
Glasgow 47J4
Glastonbury 15E7
Glazov 22L4
Glendale 46E5
Glendale 49C3
Glen Innes 42E2
Glenrothes 16F4
Glens Falls 48E1
Gliwice 13Q5
Globe 46E5
Głogów 13P5
Glomfjord 10H3
Gloucester 15E7
Gloucester 42E3
Gloucester 48F1
Gloversville 48D1
Głubczyce 13P5
Glubokoye 27H1
Gmünd 13O6
Gmunden 13N7
Gniezno 13P4
Goba 34E3
Gobabis 36D2
Gobi *des.* 27J2
Gochas 36D3
Godalming 15G7
Godavari r. 27H5
Godmanchester 15G6
Gods r. 45I4
Göhköy 23J8
Gokwe 35C5
Gołańcz 13P4
Goiana 53L5
Goiandira 55A2
Goiânia 55A2
Goiás 55A2
Goiás *state* 55A2
Goio-Erê 54F2
Gökçeada i. 21K4
Gölcük 21N4
Gold Coast 42F1
Golden Bay 43D5
Goldsboro 47L4
Gōle 23I8
Goleta 49C3
Golköy 23H8
Golmud 27J3
Gölpazarı 21N4
Goma 34C4
Gombe 32E3
Gomera i. 32B2
Gómez Palacio 46G6
Gonaïves 51J5
Gonbad-e Kavus 26E3
Gonder 34D2
Gondia 27H4
Gongan 30B3
Gongola r. 32E3
Goole 14G5
Goondiwindi 42E1
Göppingen 13L6
Gorakhpur 27H4
Gördes 21M5
Goré 33E4
Gorgān 26E3
Gorizia 20E2
Görlitz 13O5
Gorna Oryakhovitsa 21K3
Gornji Milanovac 21I2
Gornji Vakuf 20G3
Gorno-Altaysk 27J1
Gornozavodsk 30J3
Gornyak 24J4
Gornyy 23J6
Gorodets 23J6
Gorodishche 23J6
Gorodovikovsk 23I7
Gorokhovets 22I4
Gorom Gorom 32C3
Gorontalo 29E7
Gorshechnoye 23H6
Goryachiy Klyuch 23H7
Gorzów Wielkopolski 13O4
Gosford 14F3
Goshen 48D1
Gosište 40C5
Gospić 20F2
Gosport 15F8
Gossi 32C3
Götene 11H7
Gotha 13M5
Gothenburg 11G8
Gotland i. 11K8
Gotse Delchev 21J4
Götsu 31D6
Göttingen 13L5
Gouda 12J4
Gouin, Réservoir *resr* 45K5
Goulburn 42D5
Goundam 32C3
Gouraya 19G5
Gourcy 32C3
Gouré 32E3
Governador Valadares 55C2
Goya 54E3
Göyçay 23J8
Gozo i. 20F6
Graaff-Reinet 36G7
Grabouw 36D8
Gračac 20F2
Grafton 42D3
Grafton 48A3
Graham 46H5
Grahamstown 37H7
Grajaú 53I5
Grampian Mountains 16E4
Granada 19E3
Granada 51G6
Granby 45K5
Gran Canaria i. 32B2
Gran Chaco *reg.* 54D3
Grand Bahama i. 47L6
Grand Bank 45M5
Grand Banks of Newfoundland *sea feature* 48L5
Grand-Bassam 32C4
Grand Canyon *gorge* 49F2
Grand Cayman i. 51H5
Grande, Bahía b. 54C8
Grande Prairie 44G4
Grand Erg de Bilma *des.* 32E3
Grand Erg Occidental *des.* 32D2
Grand Erg Oriental *des.* 32D2
Grandes, Salinas *salt marsh* 54D4
Grand Falls-Windsor 45M5
Grand Forks 47H2
Grand Island 46H3
Grand Junction 46F4
Grand-Lahou 32C4
Grândola 19B4
Grand Rapids 47J2
Grand Rapids 47J3
Grand Turk 51J4
Grängesberg 11I6
Granja 53J4
Gränna 11I7
Grantham 15G6
Grantown-on-Spey 16F3
Grants 46F4
Grants Pass 46C3
Grantville 48C2
Granville 18D2
Grão Mogol 55C2
Graskop 37J3
Grasse 18H5
Graus 19G2
Gravatai 55A5
Gravesend 15H7
Gravina in Puglia 20G4
Grays 15H7
Graz 13O7
Great Abaco i. 47L6
Great Australian Bight g. 40F6
Great Bahama Bank *sea feature* 47L6
Great Barrier Island 43E3
Great Barrier Reef *reef* 41J2
Great Basin 46D4
Great Bear Lake 44G3
Great Belt *sea chan.* 11G9
Great Bend 46H4
Great Britain i. 12G4
Great Dividing Range *mts* 42B6
Greater Antilles *is* 51H4
Great Exuma i. 47L7
Great Falls 46E2
Great Inagua i. 47M7
Great Karoo *plat.* 36F7
Great Limpopo Transfrontier Park *nat. park* 37J2
Great Malvern 15E6
Great Nicobar i. 27I6
Great Ouse r. 15H6
Great Rift Valley *valley* 34D4
Great Salt Lake 46E3
Great Salt Lake Desert 46E3
Great Sand Sea *des.* 33F2
Great Sandy Desert 40E4
Great Slave Lake 44G3
Great Stour r. 15I7
Great Torrington 15C8
Great Victoria Desert 40F5
Great Waltham 15H7
Great Yarmouth 15I6
Greece *country* 21I5
Greeley 46F3
Green Bay 47J3
Greenfield 48F1
Greenland *terr.* 45N2
Greenland Sea 24A2
Greenock 16E5
Green River 46F3
Greensburg 48B2
Greenville 47I5
Greenville 47J5
Greenville 47K5
Greenwich 48E2
Greenwood 47K5

Gregory Range *hills* 41I3
Greifswald 13N3
Grená 11I8
Grenada 47J5
Grenada *country* 51L6
Grenfell 42D4
Grenoble 18G4
Gosforth 14F3
Gretna 16F6
Grevena 21I4
Greybull 46F3
Greymouth 43C6
Grey Range *hills* 42A2
Gribanovskiy 23I6
Griffin 47J5
Griffith 42C5
Grimari 34B3
Grimsby 14G5
Grimshaw 44G4
Grimstad 11F7
Grindavík 10□ 2
Grindsted 11F9
Grmeč *mts* 20G2
Groblersdal 37I3
Groningen 13K4
Groote Eylandt i. 41H2
Grootfontein 35B5
Groot Swartberge *mts* 36F7
Grootvloer *salt pan* 36E5
Grosseto 20D3
Groß-Gerau 13L6
Großglockner *mt.* 13N7
Grover Beach 49B3
Groznyy 23J8
Grubišno Polje 20G2
Grudziądz 13Q4
Gryazi 23H5
Gryazovets 22I4
Gryfice 13O4
Gryfino 13O4
Guadalajara 19E3
Guadalajara 50D4
Guadalcanal i. 41M1
Guadalquivir r. 19C5
Guadalupe Victoria 46G7
Guadarrama, Sierra de *mts* 19D3
Guadeloupe *terr.* 51L5
Guadix 19E5
Guaíba 55A5
Guaíra 54F2
Gualeguay 54E4
Gualeguaychu 54E4
Guam *terr.* 29G6
Guamúchil 46F6
Guanajuato 50D4
Guanambi 55C1
Guanare 52E2
Guane 51H4
Guangyuan 27J3
Guangzhou 27K4
Guanhães 55C2
Guantánamo 51I4
Guapé 55B3
Guaporé 55A5
Guaporé r. 52E6
Guarabira 53L5
Guaranda 52C4
Guarapari 55C3
Guarapuava 55A4
Guararapes 55A3
Guaratinguetá 55B3
Guaratuba 55A4
Guarda 19C3
Guárujá 55B3
Guasave 46F6
Guatemala 50F6
Guatemala *country* 50F5
Guaxupé 55B3
Guayaquil 52C4
Guayaquil, Golfo de g. 52B4
Guaymas 46E6
Guben 13O4
Gudermes 23J8
Guéckédou 32B4
Guelma 20B6
Guelmine 32B2
Guelph 48A1
Guéret 18E3
Guernsey *terr.* 15E9
Guérou 32B3
Guider 33E4
Guidonia-Montecelio 20E4
Guiglo 32C4
Guildford 15G7
Guilin 27J4
Guimarães 19B3
Guimarães 53J4
Guinea *country* 32B3
Guinea, Gulf of 32D4
Guinea-Bissau *country* 32B3
Güines 51H4
Guiratinga 53H7
Guiyang 27J4
Gujanwala 27G3
Gukovo 23H6
Gulbarga 27G5
Gulbene 11O8
Gulfport 47J5
Guliston 26F2
Gul'kevichi 23I7
Gulu 34D3
Gumare 35C5
Gumel 32D3
Guna 27G4
Gundagai 42D5
Güney 21M5
Gunnison 46F4
Guntakal 27G5
Gunungsitoli 29B7
Gurinhatã 55A2
Gurupá 53H4
Gurupi 53I6
Gur'yevsk 11L9
Gusau 32D3
Gusev 11M9
Gushan 31A5
Gusinoozersk 25L4
Gus'-Khrustal'nyy 22I5
Güstrow 13M4
Gütersloh 13L5
Guwahati 27I4
Guyana *country* 53G2
Guymon 46G4
Guyra 42E3

Gvardeysk 11L9
Gwalior 27G4
Gwanda 35C6
Gwardafuy, Gees c. 34F2
Gweru 35C5
Gweta 35C6
Gyangzê 27I4
Gydan Peninsula 24I2
Gympie 41K5
Gyöngyös 13Q7
Győr 13P7
Gytheio 21J6
Gyula 21I1
Gyumri 23I8

Haapsalu 11M7
Haarlem 12J4
Habbān 34E2

Koutiala 32C3
Kouvola 11O6
Kovdor 10Q3
Kovel' 23E6
Kovernino 22I4
Kovrov 22I4
Kovylkino 23I5
Kowanyama 41I3
Köyceğiz 21M6
Kozani 21I4
Kozara mts 20G2
Kozelets' 23F6
Kozel'sk 23G5
Kozlu 21N4
Koz'modem'yansk 22J4
Kožuf mts 21J4
Kozyatyn 23F6
Kpalimé 32D4
Krabi 29B7
Krâchéh 29C6
Kragerø 11F7
Kragujevac 21I2
Kraków 13Q5
Kramators'k 23H6
Kramfors 10J5
Kranidi 21J6
Kranj 20F1
Krāslava 11O9
Krasnaya Gorbatka 22I5
Krasnoarmeysk 23J6
Krasnoarmiys'k 23H6
Krasnoborsk 22J3
Krasnodar 23H7
Krasnodon 23H6
Krasnogorodskoye 11P8
Krasnogvardeyskoye 23I7
Krasnohrad 23G6
Krasnohvardiys'ke 23G7
Krasnoperekops'k 23G7
Krasnoslobodsk 23I5
Krasnoyarsk 24K4
Krasnyy 23F5
Krasnyye Baki 22J4
Krasnyy Kholm 22H4
Krasnyy Kut 23J6
Krasnyy Luch 23H6
Krasnyy Lyman 23H6
Krasnyy Yar 23K7
Krasyliv 23E6
Krefeld 13K5
Kremenchuk 23G6
Krems an der Donau 13O6
Kresttsy 22G4
Kretinga 11L9
Kribi 32D4
Kristiansand 11E7
Kristianstad 11I8
Kristiansund 10E5
Kristinehamn 11I7
Kritiko Pelagos sea 21K6
Krk i. 20F2
Krolevets' 23G6
Kronshtadt 11P7
Kroonstad 37H4
Kropotkin 23I7
Krosno 23D6
Krotoszyn 13P5
Krui 29C8
Krumovgrad 21K4
Krupki 23F5
Kruševac 21I3
Krychaw 23F5
Krymsk 23H7
Kryvyy Rih 23G7
Ksar Chellala 19H6
Ksar el Boukhari 19H6
Ksar el Kebir 19D6
Ksour Essaf 20D7
Kstovo 22J4
Kuala Lipis 29C7
Kuala Lumpur 29C7
Kuala Terengganu 29C7
Kuandian 30B4
Kuantan 29C7
Kubrat 21L3
Kuching 29D7
Kuçovë 21H4
Kudat 29D7
Kufstein 13N7
Kugesi 22J4
Kuhmo 10P4
Kuito 35B5
Kujang 31B5
Kuji 31F4
Kukës 21I3
Kukmor 22K4
Kula 21M5
Kular 25O2
Kuldīga 11L8
Kulebaki 23I5
Kulmbach 13M5
Kŭlob 27F3
Kul'sary 26E2
Kulunda 24I4
Kumagaya 31E5
Kumamoto 31C6
Kumano 31E6
Kumanovo 21I3
Kumasi 32C4
Kumba 32D4
Kumdah 34E1
Kumeny 22K4
Kumertau 24G4
Kumi 31C5
Kumi 33G4
Kumla 11I7
Kumo 32E3
Kumylzhenskiy 23I6
Kungälv 11G8
Kungsbacka 11H8
Kunlun Shan mts 27G3
Kunming 27J4
Kunsan 31B6
Kuopio 10O5
Kupang 40E2
Kupiškis 11N9
Kup"yans'k 23H6
Kuqa 27H2
Kurashiki 31D6
Kurayoshi 31D6
Kurchatov 23G6
Kŭrdzhali 21K4
Kure 31D6
Kuressaare 11M7
Kurgan 24H4
Kurganinsk 23I7
Kurikka 10M5
Kuril Islands 30H3
Kurkino 23H5
Kurmuk 33G3
Kurnool 27G5
Kuroiso 31F5
Kurri Kurri 42E4
Kursavka 23I7
Kursk 23H6
Kurskaya 23J7
Kurşunlu 23G8
Kuruman 36F4
Kurume 31C6
Kurunegala 27H6
Kuşadası 21L6
Kushchevskaya 23H7
Kushiro 30G4
Kushmurun 26F1
Kusŏng 31B5
Kütahya 21M5
K'ut'aisi 23I8
Kutjevo 20G2
Kutno 13Q4
Kutu 34B4
Kutztown 48D2
Kuusamo 10P4
Kuusankoski 11O6
Kuvshinovo 22G4
Kuwait 26D4
Kuwait country 26D4
Kuybyshev 24I4
Kuybysheve 23H7
Kuybyshevskoye Vodokhranilishche resr 23K5
Kuytun 27H2
Kuyucak 21M6
Kuznetsk 23J5
Kuznetsovs'k 23E6
Kuzovatovo 23J5
Kvarnerić sea chan. 20F2
Kwale 32D4
KwaMashu 37J5
Kwa Mtoro 35D4
Kwangju 31B6
Kwanobuhle 37G7
Kwatinidubu 37H7
KwaZulu-Natal prov. 37J5
Kwekwe 35C5
Kweneng admin. dist. 36G2
Kwidzyn 13Q4
Kyakhta 25L4
Kyaukpyu 27I5
Kymi 21K5
Kyneton 42B6
Kyogle 42F2
Kyŏngju 31C6
Kyōto 31D6
Kyparissia 21I6
Kyrgyzstan country 27G2
Kythira i. 21J6
Kyūshū i. 31C7
Kyustendil 21J3
Kyzyl 24K4
Kyzylkum Desert 26F2
Kyzyl-Mazhalyk 24K4
Kyzylorda 26F2

L

Laagri 11N7
Laâyoune 32B2
La Banda 54D3
Labasa 39H3
Labé 32B3
Labinsk 23I7
Labouheyre 18D4
Laboulaye 54D4
Labrador reg. 45L4
Labrador City 45L4
Labrador Sea 45M3
Lábrea 52F5
Labuhanbilik 27J6
Labuna 29E8
Labytnangi 24H3
La Carlota 54D4
Laccadive Islands 27G5
Lac du Bonnet 47H1
La Ceiba 51G5
Lachlan r. 42A5
La Chorrera 51I7
Lachute 45K5
La Ciotat 18G5
Lac La Biche 44G4
Laconia 48F1
La Crosse 47I3
Ladainha 55C2
La Déroute, Passage de strait 15E9
Ladik 23G8
Ladoga, Lake 11Q6
Ladysmith 37I5
Lae 38E2
Lafayette 47I5
Lafayette 47J3
Lafia 32D4
Lafiagi 32D4
La Flèche 18D3
La Galite, Canal de sea chan. 20C6
Lagan' 23J7
Lagan r. 17G3
Lagarto 53K6
Lågen r. 11G7
Laghouat 32D1
Lago Agrio 52C3
Lagoa Santa 55C2
Lagoa Vermelha 55A5
Lagos 19B5
Lagos 32D4
Lagosa 35C4
La Grande 46D2
La Grande 4, Réservoir resr 45K4
La Grange 47J5
La Gran Sabana plat. 52F2
Laguna 55A5
Laha 30B2
La Habra 49D4
Lahad Datu 29D7
La Hague, Cap de c. 15F9
Lahat 29C8
Laḥij 34E2
Laholm 11H8
Lahore 27G3
Lahti 11N6
Laï 33E4
Laidley 42F1
Laihia 10M5
L'Aïr, Massif de mts 32D3
Laishevo 22K5
Laitila 11L6
Laiyang 28E4
Laizhou Wan b. 27K3
Lajeado 55A5
Lajes 53K5
Lajes 55A4
La Junta 46G4
La Juventud, Isla de i. 51H4
Lake Cargelligo 42C4
Lake Charles 47I5
Lake City 47K5
Lake Havasu City 49E3
Lakehurst 48D2
Lakeland 47K6
Lake Providence 47I5
Lakes Entrance 42D6
Lakeside 48C4
Lakewood 48B1
Lakewood 48D2
Lakhdenpokh'ya 10Q6
Lakota 32C4
Laksefjorden sea chan. 10O1
La Ligua 54B4
Lalín 19B2
La Línea de la Concepción 19D5
Lalitpur 27G4
La Louvière 12J5
Lamar 46G4
La Martre, Lac l. 44G3
Lambaréné 34B4
Lambayeque 52C5
Lambert's Bay 36D7
Lambeth 48A1
Lamego 19C3
La Merced 52C6
La Merced 54C3
Lamesa 46G5
La Mesa 49D4
Lamia 21J5
Lammermuir Hills 16G5
Lamont 49C3
Lampang 29B6
Lampazos 46G6
Lamu 34E4
Lancaster 14E4
Lancaster 47K5
Lancaster 48C2
Lancaster 49C3
Lancaster Sound strait 45J2
Landeck 13M7
Lander 46F3
Landsberg am Lech 13M6
Land's End pt 15B8
Landshut 13N6
Landskrona 11H9
Langenthal 18H3
Langjökull ice cap 10□ 2
Langport 15E7
Langres 18G3
Langsa 27I6
Långsele 10J5
Lannion 18C2
Lansing 47K3
Lanxi 30B3
Lanzarote i. 32B2
Lanzhou 27J3
Laoag 29E6
Lao Cai 27J4
Laon 18F2
La Oroya 52C6
Laos country 29C6
Laotougou 30C4
Lapa 55A4
La Palma 51I7
La Palma i. 32B2
La Paz 46E7
La Paz 50G6
La Paz 52E7
La Paz 54E4
La Pérouse Strait strait 30F3
La Plata 54E4
La Plata, Río de sea chan. 54E4
Lappeenranta 11P6
Lappland reg. 10K3
Lâpseki 21L4
Laptev Sea 25N2
Lapua 10M5
La Quiaca 54C2
L'Aquila 20E3
La Quinta 49D4
Larache 19C6
Laramie 46F3
Laranjal Paulista 55B3
Laranjeiras do Sul 54F3
Larba 19H5
Laredo 46H6
Largs 16E5
L'Ariana 20D6
La Rioja 54C3
La Rioja aut. comm. 19E2
Larisa 21J5
Larne 17G3
La Rochelle 18D3
La Roche-sur-Yon 18D3
La Romana 51K5
La Ronge 44H4
La Ronge, Lac l. 44H4
Larvik 11G7
Las Cruces 46F5
La Serena 54B3
Las Flores 54E5
Las Heras 54C4
Las Palmas de Gran Canaria 32B2
La Spezia 20C2
Las Tablas 51H7
Las Termas 54D3
Las Tunas 51I4
Las Varas 50C4
Las Varillas 54D4
Las Vegas 46F4
Las Vegas 49E2
Latacunga 52C4
Latakia 33G1
La Teste-de-Buch 18D4
Latina 20E4
La Tuque 47M2
Latvia country 11N8
Lauchhammer 13N5
Launceston 15C8
Launceston 41J8
Laurel 47J5
Laureldale 48D2
Laurel Hill hills 48B3
Laurinburg 47L5
Lausanne 18H3
Lautoka 39H3
Laval 18D2
La Vall d'Uixó 19F4
La Vega 51J5
Lavras 55B3
Lawra 32C3
Lawrence 47H4
Lawrence 48F1
Lawrenceburg 47J4
Lawton 46H5
Lazarev 30F1
Lazarevac 21I2
Lázaro Cárdenas 50D5
Lazdijai 11M9
Leamington Spa, Royal 15F6
Leatherhead 15G7
Lebanon 47I4
Lebanon 48C2
Lebanon 48E1
Lebanon country 33G1
Lebedyan' 23H5
Lębork 13P3
Lebowakgomo 37I3
Lebrija 19C5
Lebu 54B5
Lecce 20H4
Lecco 20C2
Lechaina 21I6
Le Creusot 18G3
Le Crotoy 15I8
Ledesma 19D3
Ledmozero 10R4
Leeds 14F5
Leek 15E5
Leesburg 48C3
Leesville 47I5
Leeuwarden 13J4
Leeuwin, Cape 40D6
Leeward Islands 51L5
Lefkada 21I5
Lefkada i. 21I5
Lefkimmi 21I5
Legnago 20D2
Legnica 13P5
Le Havre 15H9
Lehmo 10P5
Leibnitz 13O7
Leicester 15F6
Leiden 12J4
Leigh 14E5
Leigh Creek 41H6
Leighton Buzzard 15G7
Leipzig 13N5
Leiria 19B4
Leirvik 11D7
Leizhou Bandao pen. 27J4
Le Kef 20C6
Leksand 11I6
Lelystad 12J4
Le Mans 18E2
Le Mars 47H3
Leme 55B3
Lemmon 46G2
Lemoore 49C2
Le Murge hills 20G4
Lemvig 11F8
Lena r. 25N2
Lenham 15H7
Lenine 23G7
Leningradskaya 23H7
Leningradskaya Oblast' admin. div. 11R7
Leningradskiy 25S3
Leninsk 23J6
Leninskiy 23H5
Leninsk-Kuznetskiy 24J4
Leninskoye 22J4
Leninskoye 30D3
Lens 18F1
Lensk 25M3
Lenti 20G1
Lentini 20F6
Léo 32C3
Leoben 13O7
Leominster 15E6
Leominster 48F1
León 19D2
León 50D4
León 51G6
Leongatha 42B7
Leonidio 21J6
Leonidovo 30F2
Leonora 40E5
Leopoldina 55C3
Lepontine, Alpi mts 18I3
Le Puy-en-Velay 18F4
Lerala 37H2
Léré 32C3
Lerma 19E2
Le Roy 48C1
Lerum 11H8
Lerwick 16□
Lesbos i. 21K5
Les Cayes 51J5
Leshan 27J4
Leshukonskoye 22J2
Leskovac 21I3
Lesosibirsk 24K4
Lesotho country 37I5
Lesozavodsk 30D3
L'Espérance Rock i. 39I5
Les Sables-d'Olonne 18D3
Lesser Antilles is 51K6
Lesser Caucasus mts 23I8
Lesser Slave Lake 44G4
Leszno 13P5
Letchworth Garden City 15G7
Lethbridge 44G5
Leticia 52E4
Letnerechenskiy 22G2
Le Touquet-Paris-Plage 15I8
Letterkenny 17E3
Leuchars 16G4
Leuven 12J5
Levanger 10G5
Levashi 23J8
Levelland 46G5
Leven 14G5
Leven, Loch l. 16F4
Lévêque, Cape 40E3
Leverkusen 13K5
Levice 13Q6
Levittown 48D2
Levittown 48E2
Lev Tolstoy 23H5
Lewes 15H8
Lewis, Isle of i. 16C2
Lewisburg 48C2
Lewis Range mts 46E2
Lewiston 46D2
Lewistown 46F2
Lewistown 48C2
Lexington 46H3
Lexington 47K4
Lexington 48B4
Lezhë 21H4
L'gov 23G6
Lhasa 27I4
Lianyungang 28D4
Liaodong Wan b. 27L2
Liaoning prov. 30A4
Liaoyang 30A4
Liaoyuan 30B4
Liaozhong 30A4
Libenge 34B3
Liberal 46G4
Liberec 13O5
Liberia 51G6
Liberia country 32C4
Libourne 18D4
Libreville 34A3
Libya country 33E2
Libyan Desert 33F2
Libyan Plateau 33F1
Licata 20E6
Lichfield 15F6
Lichinga 35D5
Lichtenburg 37H4
Lida 11N10
Lidköping 11H7
Liebig, Mount 40G4
Liechtenstein country 18I3
Liège 13J5
Lieksa 10Q5
Lienz 13N7
Liepāja 11L8
Liezen 13O7
Liffey r. 17F4
Lifford 17E3
Lightning Ridge 42C2
Ligurian Sea 18I5
Lika reg. 20F2
Likasi 35C5
Likhoslavl' 22G4
Lilla Edet 11H7
Lille 18F1
Lillehammer 11G6
Lillestrøm 11G7
Lilongwe 35D5
Lima 47K3
Lima 48C1
Lima 52C6
Lima Duarte 55C3
Liman 23J7
Limassol 33G1
Limavady 17F2
Limbaži 11N8
Limeira 55B3
Limerick 17D5
Limmen Bight b. 41H2
Limnos i. 21K5
Limoeiro 53K5
Limoges 18E4
Limon 46G4
Limoux 18F5
Limpopo prov. 37I2
Limpopo r. 37K3
Limpopo National Park 37J2
Linares 19E4
Linares 46H7
Linares 54B5
Lincoln 14G5
Lincoln 47H3
Lincoln 47J3
Lincoln 54D4
Lindau (Bodensee) 13L7
Linden 53G2
Lindi 35D4
Lindian 30B3
Line Islands 6
Linfen 27K3
Lingen (Ems) 13K4
Lingga, Kepulauan is 29C8
Linhares 55C2
Linhe 27J2
Linjiang 30B4
Linköping 11I7
Linkou 30C3
Linlithgow 16F5
Linnhe, Loch inlet 16D4
Lins 55A3
Linxi 27K2
Linxia 27J3
Linyi 27K3
Linz 13O6
Lion, Golfe du g. 18F5
Lipetsk 23H5
Lipova 21I1
Lira 34D3
Lisala 34C3
Lisbon 19B4
Lisburn 17F3
Lishu 30B4
Lisieux 18E2
Liski 23H6
Lismore 42F2
Lithgow 42E4
Lithuania country 11M9
Litoměřice 13O5
Little Andaman i. 27I5
Little Belt sea chan. 11F9
Little Cayman i. 51H5
Little Falls 47I2
Littlefield 46G5
Littlehampton 15G8
Little Minch sea chan. 16B3
Little Rock 47I5
Liuhe 30B4
Liuzhou 27J4
Livadeia 21J5
Livermore 49B2
Liverpool 14E5
Liverpool 42E4
Liverpool Plains 42E3
Liverpool Range mts 42D3
Livingston 16F5
Livingston 46E2
Livingston 47I5
Livingstone 35C5
Livno 20G3
Livny 23H5
Livorno 20D3
Livramento do Brumado 55C1
Lizard Point 15B9
Ljubljana 20F1
Ljungby 11H8
Ljusdal 11J6
Llandovery 15D7
Llandudno 14D5
Llanelli 15C7
Llangollen 15D6
Llano Estacado plain 46G5
Llanos plain 52E2
Llantrisant 15D7
Llay 15D5
Lleida 19G3
Llodio 19E2
Lobatse 37G3
Loberia 54E5
Lobito 35B5
Lobos 54E5
Lochy, Loch l. 16E4
Lockerbie 16F5
Lock Haven 48C2
Lockport 48B1
Lodeynoye Pole 22G3
Lodi 20C2
Lodi 49B1
Lodja 34C4
Łódź 13Q5
Lofoten is 10H2
Log 23I6
Logan 46E3
Logan, Mount 44D3
Logatec 20F2
Logroño 19E2
Loimaa 11M6
Loire r. 18C3
Loja 19D5
Loja 52C4
Løkken 10F5
Loknya 22F4
Lokoja 32D4
Lokossa 32D4
Lokot' 23G5
Lolland i. 11G9
Lom 21J3
Lomas de Zamora 54E4
Lombok i. 40D1
Lombok, Selat sea chan. 29D8
Lomé 32D4
Lomond, Loch l. 16E4
Lomonosov 11P7
Lompoc 49B3
Łomża 13S4
London 15G7
London 47K4
London 48A1
Londonderry 17E3
Londonderry, Cape 40F2
Londrina 55A3
Longa, Proliv sea chan. 25S2
Long Ashton 15E7
Long Beach 49C4
Long Branch 48E2
Long Eaton 15F6
Longford 17E4
Long Island 48E2
Long Island Sound sea chan. 48E2
Longjiang 30A3
Longmeadow 48E1
Long Melford 15H6
Longmont 46F3
Long Point Bay 48A1
Longreach 41I4
Longtown 14E3
Longview 47I5
Long Xuyên 29C6
Longyan 28D5
Longyearbyen 24C2
Lönsboda 11I8
Lons-le-Saunier 18G3
Lop Buri 29C6
Lop Nur salt flat 27I2
Lorain 45J5
Lorca 19F5
Lord Howe Island 41L6
Lorena 55B3
Loreto 53I5
Lorient 18C3
Lorn, Firth of est. 16D4
Lorrain, Plateau 18H2
Los Alamos 46F4
Los Angeles 49C3
Los Ángeles 54B5
Los Banos 49B2
Los Chonos, Archipiélago de is 54A6
Los Juríes 54D3
Los Mochis 46F6
Lossiemouth 16F3
Los Teques 52E1
Lostwithiel 15C8
Los Vilos 54B4
Lot r. 18E4
Lota 54B5
Louangnamtha 28C5
Louangphabang 29C6
Loubomo 35B4
Louga 32B3
Loughborough 15F6
Loughrea 17D4
Loughton 15H7
Louisiade Archipelago is 41K2
Louisiana state 47I5
Louisville 47J4
Loukhi 10R3
Loulé 19B5
Loum 32D4
Louny 13N5
Lourdes 18D5
Louth 14G5
Loutra Aidipsou 21J5
Lovech 21K3
Loviisa 11O6
Lovington 46G5
Lowell 48F1
Lower Hutt 43E5
Lower Lough Erne l. 17E3
Lowestoft 15I6
Łowicz 13Q4
Loxton 41I6
Loyauté, Îles is 39G4
Loyew 23F6
Loznica 21H2
Lozova 23H6
Luanda 35B4
Luanshya 35C5
Luau 35C5
Luba 32D4
Lubaczów 23D6
Lubango 35B5
Lubao 35C4
Lubartów 23D6
Lubbock 46G5
Lübeck 13M4
Lubin 13P5
Lublin 23D6
Lubny 23G6
Lubumbashi 35C5
Lucala 35B4
Lucapa 35C4
Lucca 20D3
Luce Bay 16E6
Lucélia 55A3
Lucena 19D5
Lucena 29E6
Lučenec 13Q6
Lucera 20F4
Lucerne 18I3
Luchegorsk 30D3
Luckenwalde 13N4
Lucknow 27H4
Lüdenscheid 13K5
Lüderitz 36B4
Ludhiana 27G3
Ludvika 11I6
Ludwigsburg 13L6
Ludwigshafen am Rhein 13L6
Ludza 11O8
Luebo 35C4
Luena 35B5
Lufkin 47I5
Luga 11P7
Lugano 18I3
Lugo 19C2
Lugo 20D2
Lugoj 21I2
Luhans'k 23H6
Lukhovitsy 23H5
Lukovit 21K3
Łuków 23D6
Lukoyanov 23J5
Luleå 10M4
Luleälven r. 10M4
Lüleburgaz 21L4
Lumberton 47L5
Lumbrales 19C3
Lumezzane 20D2
Lund 11H9
Lundy i. 15C7
Lune r. 14E4
Lüneburg 13M4
Lunéville 18H2
Luninyets 11O10
Lunsar 32B4
Luobei 30C3
Luohe 27K3
Luoyang 27K3
Lupane 35C5
Lupanshui 27J4
Lupeni 21J2
Lurgan 17F3
Lusaka 35C5
Lusambo 35C4
Lushnjë 21H4
Lut, Dasht-e des. 26E3
Lutherstadt Wittenberg 13N5
Luton 15G7
Luts'k 23E6
Lutzville 36D6
Luwero 34D3
Luwuk 29E8
Luxembourg 13K6
Luxembourg country 13K6
Luxor 33G2
Luza 22J3
Luzhou 27J4
Luziânia 55B2
Luzon i. 29E6
Luzon Strait strait 29E5
L'viv 23E6
Lyakhavichy 11O10
Lycksele 10K4
Lydd 15H8
Lyel'chytsy 23F6
Lyepyel' 11P9
Lyme Bay 15E8
Lyme Regis 15E8
Lymington 15F8
Lynchburg 48B4
Lynn 48F1
Lyon 18G4
Lyozna 23F5
Lysekil 11G7
Lyskovo 22J4
Lys'va 24G4
Lysychans'k 23H6
Lysyye Gory 23J6
Lytham St Anne's 14D5
Lyuban' 11P10
Lyubim 22I4
Lyudinovo 23G5

M

Ma'ān 33G1
Maastricht 13J5
Mabaruma 52G2
Mablethorpe 14H5
Mabopane 37I3
Macaé 55C3
Macajuba 55C1
Macao 27K4
Macapá 53H3
Macará 52C4
Macarani 55C1
Macas 52C4
Macau 53K5
Macclesfield 14E5
Macdonnell Ranges mts 40G4
Macduff 16G3
Macedonia country 21I4
Maceió 53K5
Macenta 32C4
Macerata 20E3
Machachi 52C4
Machakos 34D4
Machala 52C4
Machilipatnam 27H5
Machiques 52D1
Machu Picchu tourist site 52D6
Machynlleth 15D6
Măcin 21M2
Macintyre Brook r. 42E2
Maçka 23H8
Mackay 41J4
Mackenzie r. 44E3
Mackenzie Bay 44E3
Mackenzie Mountains 44E3
Macksville 42F3
Maclean 42F2
Macomb 47I3
Mâcon 18G3
Macon 47I4
Macon 47K5
Madadeni 37J4
Madagascar country 35E6
Madan 21K4
Madang 38E2
Madaoua 32D3
Madeira r. 52G4
Madeira terr. 32B1
Madera 46F6
Madgaon 27G5
Madingou 35B4
Madison 47H3
Madison 47J3
Madison 47J4
Madison Heights 48B4
Madisonville 47J4
Madona 11O8
Madra Dağı mts 21L5
Madrakah 33G2
Madre, Laguna lag. 47H6
Madre del Sur, Sierra mts 50D5
Madre Occidental, Sierra mts 46F6
Madre Oriental, Sierra mts 46G6
Madrid 19E3
Madurai 27G6
Maebashi 31E5
Maevatanana 35E5
Mafeteng 37H5
Maffra 42C6
Mafinga 35D4
Mafra 55A4
Magabeni 37J6
Magadan 25Q4
Magangue 52D2
Magaria 32D3
Magas 23J8
Magdagachi 30B1
Magdalena 46E5
Magdeburg 13M4
Magellan, Strait of 54B8
Maggiore, Lake 20C2
Magherafelt 17F3
Maghnia 19F6
Maghull 14E5
Magnitogorsk 24G4
Magnolia 47I5
Mago 30F1
Magṭa' Lahjar 32B3
Magwe 27I4
Mahābād 33H1
Mahajanga 35E5
Mahalapye 37H2
Mahalevona 35E5
Mahanoro 35E5
Maha Sarakham 27J5
Mahd adh Dhahab 34E1
Mahdia 19G6
Mahdia 20D7
Mahdia 53G2
Mahenge 35D4
Mahilyow 23F5
Mahón 19I4
Maicao 52D1
Maidenhead 15G7
Maidstone 15H7
Maiduguri 32E3
Maine state 47N2
Maine, Gulf of 45L5
Mainland i. 16F1
Mainland i. 16□
Maintirano 35E5
Mainz 13L5
Maitland 42E4
Maizuru 31D6
Majene 29D8
Majorca i. 19H4
Makabana 34B4
Makale 29D8
Makanchi 27H2
Makarov 30F2
Makar'yev 22I4
Makassar 29D8
Makassar, Selat strait 29D8
Makat 26E2
Makeni 32B4
Makgadikgadi depr. 35C6
Makhachkala 23J8
Makinsk 27G1
Makiyivka 23H6
Makó 21I1
Makokou 34B3
Maksatikha 22G4
Makunguwiro 35D5
Makurdi 32D4
Malabar Coast 27G5
Malabo 32D4
Malacca, Strait of strait 29B7
Maladzyechna 11O9
Málaga 19D5
Malaita i. 39G2
Malakal 33G4
Malang 29D8
Malanje 35B4
Mälaren l. 11J7
Malargüe 54C5
Malatya 26C3
Malawi country 35D5
Malaya Vishera 22G4
Malāyer 33H1
Malaysia country 29C7
Malbork 13Q3
Maldives country 27G6
Maldon 15H7
Maldon 42B6
Maldonado 54F4
Male 7
Malgobek 23J8
Malhada 55C1
Mali country 32C3
Malili 38C2
Malindi 34E4
Malin Head 17E2
Malkara 21L4
Mallawī 33G2
Mallét 55A4
Mallow 17D5
Malmédy 13K5
Malmesbury 15E7
Malmesbury 36D7
Malmö 11H9
Malmyzh 22K4
Maloshuyka 22H3
Maloyaroslavets 23H5
Malta 11O8
Malta country 20F7
Malta Channel 20F6
Maltby 14F5
Maluku, Laut sea 29E8
Malung 11H6
Maluti Mountains 37I5
Malvern 47I5
Malyn 23F6
Malyye Derbety 23J7
Mamadysh 22K5
Mamelodi 37I3
Mamfe 32D4
Mamoré r. 52E6
Mamou 32B3
Mamuju 38B2
Man 32C4
Man, Isle of terr. 14C4
Manacapuru 52F4
Manacor 19H4
Manado 29E7
Managua 51G6
Manakara 35E6
Manama 34F1
Mananara Avaratra 35E5
Mananjary 35E6
Manassas 48C3
Manaus 52F4
Manavgat 33G1
Manchester 14E5
Manchester 48C3
Manchester 48E2
Manchester 48F1
Mandal 11E7
Mandalay 27I4
Mandalgovĭ 27J2
Mandan 46G2
Mandeville 51I5
Mandritsara 35E5
Mandsaur 27G4
Mandurah 40D6
Manduria 20G4
Mandya 27G5
Manevychi 23E6
Manfredonia 20F4
Manga 32C3
Manga 55C1
Mangai 34B4
Mangalia 21M3
Mangalore 27G5
Mangaung 37H5
Mangotsfield 15E7
Mangualde 19C3
Manhattan 47H4
Manhica 37K3
Manhuaçu 55C3
Manicouagan, Réservoir resr 45L4
Maniitsoq 45M3
Manila 29E6
Manilla 42E3
Manisa 21L5
Manistee 47J3
Manitoba prov. 45I4
Manitoba, Lake 45I4
Manitowoc 47J3
Manizales 52C2
Manja 35E6
Mankato 47I3
Mankono 32C4
Mannar, Gulf of 27G6
Mannheim 13L6
Mannington 48A3
Manp'o 30B4
Manresa 19G3
Mansa 35C5
Mansa Konko 32B3
Mansfield 15F5
Mansfield 42C6
Mansfield 47I5
Mansfield 47K3
Manta 52B4
Manteca 49B2
Mantena 55C2
Mantes-la-Jolie 18E2
Mantiqueira, Serra da mts 55B3
Mantoudi 21J5
Mäntsälä 11N6
Mänttä 10N5
Mantua 20D2
Manturovo 22J4
Manuel Ribas 55A4
Manuel Vitorino 55C1
Manukau 43E3
Manyas 21L4
Manyoni 35D4
Manzanillo 50D5
Manzanillo 51I4
Manzhouli 27K2
Manzini 37J4
Mao 33E3
Maokeng 37H4
Maple Creek 46F2
Maputo 37K3
Maputo prov. 37K3
Maputsoe 37H5
Maqṭeïr reg. 32B2
Maquela do Zombo 35B4
Maraã 52E4
Marabá 53I5
Maracaibo 52D1
Maracaibo, Lake 52D2
Maracaju 54E2
Maracás 55C1
Maracay 52E1
Maradi 32D3
Marajó, Ilha de i. 53H4
Marand 26D3
Marañón r. 52D4
Maraú 55D1
Marbella 19D5
Marble Hall 37I3
Marburg 37J6
Marburg an der Lahn 13L5
Marcali 20G1
March 15H6
Marcona 52C7
Mardan 27G3
Mar del Plata 54E5
Mardın 33H1
Maree, Loch l. 16D3
Margate 15I7
Margherita Peak 34C3
Marg'ilon 27G2
Marhanets' 23G7
Mariana 55C3
Marianna 47I5
Marianna 47J5
Ma'rib 34E2
Maribor 20F1
Mariehamn 11K6
Mariental 36C3
Mariestad 11H7
Marietta 47K5
Marietta 48A3
Marignane 18G5
Mariinsk 24J4
Mariinskiy Posad 22J4
Marijampolė 11M9
Marília 55A3
Marín 19B2
Marina 49B2
Mar"ina Horka 11P10
Marinette 47J2
Maringá 55A3
Marinha Grande 19B4
Marion 47J3
Marion 47K3
Marion 47K4
Marion 47L5
Maritime Alps mts 18H4
Mariupol' 23H7
Marīvān 33H1
Marka 34E3
Market Deeping 15G6
Market Harborough 15G6
Market Weighton 14G5
Markovo 25S3
Marks 23J6
Marmande 18E4
Marmara, Sea of g. 21M4
Marmaris 21M6
Marne r. 18F2
Marne-la-Vallée 18F2
Maroantsetra 35E5
Marondera 35D5
Maroochydore 42F1
Maroua 33E3
Marovoay 35E5
Marquesas Islands 6
Marquês de Valença 55C3
Marquette 47J2
Marra, Jebel mt. 33F3
Marra, Jebel plat. 33F3
Marrakech 32C1
Marsá al 'Alam 33G2
Marsabit 34D3
Marsala 20E6
Marsá Maṭrūḥ 33F1
Marseille 18G5
Marshall 47H3
Marshall 47I4
Marshall 47I5
Marshall Islands country 6
Marshalltown 47I3
Märsta 11J7
Martapura 29D8
Martigny 18H3
Martin 13Q6
Martinho Campos 55B2
Martinique terr. 51L6
Martinsburg 48C3
Martinsville 47L4
Martos 19E5
Martuk 26E1
Maruim 53K6
Mary 26F3
Maryborough 41K5
Maryland state 48C3
Marysville 49B1
Maryville 47I3
Maryville 47K4
Masai Steppe plain 35D4
Masaka 34D4
Masan 31C6
Masasi 35D5
Mascara 19G6
Mascote 55D1
Maseru 37H5
Mashhad 26E3
Masilo 37H5
Masindi 34D3
Masjed Soleymān 33H1
Mask, Lough l. 17C4
Mason City 47I3
Massa 20D2
Massachusetts state 48E1
Massachusetts Bay 48F1
Massafra 20G4
Massango 35B4
Massawa 33G3
Massenya 33E3
Massif Central mts 18F4
Massillon 48A2
Massina 32C3
Masterton 43E5
Mastung 26F4
Mastūrah 34D1
Masty 11N10
Masuda 31C6
Masvingo 35D6
Masvingo prov. 37J1
Matabeleland South prov. 37I1
Matadi 35B4
Matagalpa 51G6
Matam 32B3
Matamey 32D3
Matamoros 46G6
Matamoros 47H6
Matane 47N2
Matanzas 47K7
Mataram 29D8
Mataró 19H3
Matā'utu 39I3
Matehuala 50D4
Matemanga 35D5
Matera 20G4
Mateur 20C6
Mathura 27G4
Mati 29E7
Matias Cardoso 55C1
Matías Romero 50E5
Matlock 15F5
Mato Grosso state 55A1
Mato Grosso, Planalto do plat. 53H7
Matosinhos 19B3
Mato Verde 55C1
Matsue 31D6
Matsumoto 31E5
Matsuyama 31D6
Matterhorn mt. 18H4
Matterhorn mt. 46D3
Maturín 52F2
Matwabeng 37H5
Mauchline 16E5
Maui i. 46□
Maun 35C5
Maunatlala 37H2
Mauritania country 32B3
Mauritius country 7
Mavinga 35C5
Mawlamyaing 27I5
Mawqaq 33H2
Mayagüez 51K5
Maya Mountains 50G5
Maybole 16E5
Maych'ew 34D2
Mayenne 18D2
Maykop 23I7
Maymanah 26F3
Mayna 23J5
Mayotte terr. 35E5
Mayskiy 23J8
Mazara del Vallo 20E6
Mazār-e Sharīf 26F3
Mazatlán 50C4
Mažeikiai 11M8
Mazyr 23F5
Mbabane 37J4
Mbahiakro 32C4
Mbaïki 34B3
Mbale 34D3
Mbalmayo 32E4
Mbandaka 34B4
M'banza Congo 35B4
Mbarara 33G5
Mbari r. 34C3
Mbeya 35D4
Mbinga 35D5
Mbouda 32E4
Mbour 32B3
Mbuji-Mayi 35C4
Mburucuyá 54E3
McAlester 47H5
McAllen 46H6
McCall 46D3
McCook 46G3
Mchinga 35D4
McKinley, Mount 44C3
McMinnville 46C2
McPherson 46H4
Mdantsane 37H7
M'Daourouch 20B6
Mead, Lake resr 49E2
Meadville 48A2
Meaux 18F2
Mecca 34D1
Mechanicsville 48C4
Mechelen 12J5
Mecheria 32C1
Mecklenburger Bucht b. 13M3
Medan 27I6
Médéa 19H5
Medellín 52C2
Medenine 32E1
Medford 46C3
Medford 48E2
Medgidia 21M2
Media 48D3
Mediaș 21K1
Medicine Bow Mountains 46F3
Medicine Hat 44G4
Medina 34D1
Medina 55C2
Medina de Rioseco 19D3
Mediterranean Sea 20D6
Medvedevo 22J4
Medvezh'yegorsk 22G3
Meekatharra 40D5
Meerut 27G4
Megalopoli 21J6
Meiganga 33E4
Meihekou 30B4
Meiktila 27I4
Meiningen 13M5
Meißen 13N5
Meixi 30C3
Meizhou 28D5
Mek'elē 34D2
Mékhé 32B3
Meknès 32C1
Mekong r. 27J4
Mekong r. 29C6
Melaka 29C7
Melbourne 42B6
Melbourne 47K6
Melenki 23I5
Melilla 19E6
Melitopol' 23G7
Melk 13O6
Melksham 15E7
Melo 54F4
Melrose 16G5
Melton 42B6
Melton Mowbray 15G6
Melun 18F2
Melville Bay 41H2
Melville Island 40G2
Melville Island 45H2
Memmingen 13M7
Memphis 47I4
Mena 23G6
Mena 47I5
Mende 18F4
Mendefera 33G3
Mendeleyevsk 22L5
Mendi 38E2
Mendip Hills 15E7
Mendoza 54C4
Menemen 21L5
Menongue 35B5
Mentawai, Kepulauan is 29B8
Menton 18H5
Menzel Bourguiba 20C6
Menzel Temime 20D6
Meppen 13K4
Meqheleng 37H5
Merano 20D1
Merauke 29G8
Merced 49B2
Mercedes 54E3
Mercedes 54E4
Mercês 55C3
Mere 15E7
Merefa 23H6
Mergui Archipelago is 27I5
Mérida 19C4
Mérida 50G4
Mérida 52D2
Meriden 48E2
Meridian 47J5
Mérignac 18D4
Merimbula 42D6
Merowe 33G3
Merredin 40D6
Merrill 47J2
Mersa Fatma 33H3
Mersey est. 14E5
Mersin 33G1
Merthyr Tydfil 15D7
Merzig 13K6
Mesa 46E5
Mesagne 20G4
Mesolongi 21I5
Mesquita 55C2
Messina 20F5
Messina, Strait of strait 20F5
Messini 21J6
Mestre 20E2
Meta r. 52E2
Metán 54C3
Methuen 48F1
Metlaoui 32D1
Metu 34D3
Metz 18H2
Meuse r. 12J5
Mevagissey 15C8
Mexicali 49E4
Mexico country 50D4
Mexico, Gulf of 47H6
Mexico City 50E5
Meyersdale 48B3
Mezdra 21J3
Mezen' 22J2
Mezen' r. 22J2
Mezhdurechensk 22K3
Mezhdurechensk 24J4
Mezőtúr 21I1
Miami 47I4
Miami 47K6
Miami Beach 47K6
Mīāndowāb 33H1
Miandrivazo 35E5
Mianwali 27G3
Mianyang 27J3
Miarinarivo 35E5
Miass 24H4
Michalovce 23D6
Michigan state 47J2
Michigan, Lake 47J3
Michurinsk 23I5
Micronesia, Federated States of country 29G7
Middelburg 12I5
Middelburg 37I3
Middelfart 11F9
Middle River 48C3
Middlesbrough 14F4
Middletown 48D2
Middletown 48E2
Midland 46G5
Midland 47L3
Midleton 17D6
Miðvágur 10□ 1
Mielec 23D6
Miercurea-Ciuc 21K1
Mieres 19D2
Miguel Auza 46G7
Mihara 31D6
Mikhaylov 23H5
Mikhaylovka 23I6
Mikhaylovka 30D4
Mikhaylovskiy 24I4
Mikkeli 11O6
Milan 20C2
Milas 21L6
Milazzo 20F5
Mildenhall 15H6
Mildura 41I6
Miles 42E1
Miles City 46F2
Milford 48F1
Milford Haven 15B7
Milford Sound inlet 43A7
Miliana 19H5
Mil'kovo 25Q4
Millau 18F4
Milledgeville 47K5
Mille Lacs, Lac des l. 45I5
Millerovo 23I6
Millmerran 42E1
Millville 48D3
Milpitas 49B2
Milton Keynes 15G6
Milwaukee 47J3
Mīnāb 26E4
Minahasa, Semenanjung pen. 29E7
Minas 27J6
Minas 54E4
Minas Gerais state 55B2
Minas Novas 55C2
Minatitlán 50F5
Mindanao i. 29E7
Mindelo 32□
Minden 13L4
Minden 47I5
Mindoro i. 29E6
Mindouli 34B4
Minehead 15D7
Mineola 48E2
Mineral'nyye Vody 23I7
Mineral Wells 46H5
Minerva 48A2
Mingäçevir 23J8
Minglanilla 19F4
Mingoyo 35D5
Mingshui 30B3
Minna 32D4
Minneapolis 47I3
Minnesota state 47I2
Minorca i. 19H3
Minot 46G2
Minsk 11O10
Mińsk Mazowiecki 13R4
Minusinsk 24K4
Mirabela 55B2
Miraí 55C3
Miramar 54E5
Miramichi 45L5
Miranda 54E2
Miranda de Ebro 19E2
Mirandela 19C3
Mirandola 20D2
Mirassol 55A3
Mirboo North 42C7
Miri 29D7
Mirim, Lagoa l. 54F4
Mirnyy 25M3
Mirpur Khas 27F4
Miryang 31C6
Mirzapur 27H4
Miskolc 23D6
Mişrātah 33E1
Mission Viejo 49D4
Mississauga 48B1
Mississippi r. 47J6
Mississippi state 47J5
Missoula 46E2
Missouri r. 47I4
Missouri state 47I4
Mistassini, Lac l. 45K4
Mistelbach 13P6
Mitchell 41J5
Mitchell 46H3
Mitchell r. 41I3
Mitchelstown 17D5
Mito 31F5
Mitrovicë 21I3
Mitú 52D3
Mitumba, Chaîne des mts 35C5
Miura 31E6
Miyako 31F5
Miyakonojō 31C7
Miyazaki 31C7
Miyazu 31D6
Miyoshi 31D6
Mizen Head 17C6
Mizhhirr"ya 23D6
Mizusawa 31F5
Mjölby 11I7
Mkata 35D4
Mladá Boleslav 13O5
Mladenovac 21I2
Mława 13R4
Mlungisi 37H6
Mmabatho 37G3
Moanda 34B4
Moberly 47I4
Mobile 47J5
Mobile Bay 47J5
Moçambique 35E5
Mocha 34E2
Mochudi 37H3
Mocimboa da Praia 35E5
Mocoa 52C3
Mococa 55B3
Mocuba 35D5
Modder r. 37G5
Modena 20D2
Modesto 49B2
Moe 42C7
Moelv 11G6
Moffat 16F5
Mogadishu 34E3
Mogi-Mirim 55B3
Mogocha 25M4
Mogoditshane 37G3
Mohács 20H2
Mohale's Hoek 37H6
Mohammadia 19G6
Mohoro 35D4
Mohyliv Podil's'kyy 23E6
Moinești 21L1
Mo i Rana 10I3
Mojave Desert 49D3
Moji das Cruzes 55B3

Ulundi 37J5
Uluṟu *hill* 40G5
Ulva *i.* 16C4
Ulverston 14D4
Ul'yanovsk 23K5
Ulysses 46G4
Uman' 23F6
Umba 22G2
Umeå 10L5
Umeälven *r.* 10L5
Umhlanga Rocks 37J5
Umlazi 37J5
Umm Ruwaba 33G3
Umtata 37I6
Umuahia 32D4
Umuarama 54F2
Una 55D1
Unaí 55B2
'Unayzah 26D4
Unecha 23G5
Ungava, Péninsule d' *pen.* 45K3
Ungava Bay 45L4
Ungheni 21L1
Ungwana Bay 34E4
Uni 22K4
União 53J4
União da Vitória 55A4
União dos Palmares 53K5
Union City 47J4
Uniontown 48B3
United Arab Emirates *country* 26E4
United Kingdom *country* 12G3
United States of America *country* 46F3
Unity 44H4
Ŭnp'a 31B5
Ŭnsan 31B5
Unst *i.* 16□
Upemba, Lac *l.* 35C4
Upernavik 45M2
Upington 36E5
Upland 49D3
Upper Hutt 43E5
Upper Lough Erne *l.* 17E3
Upper Yarra Reservoir 42B6
Uppsala 11J7
Upton 48F1
Ural *r.* 26E2
Uralla 42E3
Ural Mountains 24H3
Ural'sk 26E1
Urambo 35D4
Urandi 55C1
Urawa 31E6
Urbino 20E3
Urdoma 22K3
Uren' 22J4
Urganch 26F2
Urla 21L5
Urmia, Lake *salt l.* 26D3
Uruaçu 55A1
Uruana 55A1
Uruapan 50D5
Urubamba *r.* 52D6
Urucara 53G4
Uruçuca 55D1
Uruçuí 53J5
Urucurituba 53G4
Uruguaiana 54E3
Uruguay *country* 54E4
Uruguay *r.* 54E4
Ürümqi 27H2
Urusha 30A1
Uryupinsk 23I6
Urzhum 22K4
Urziceni 21L2
Usa 31C6
Uşak 21M5
Ushtobe 27G2
Ushuaia 54C8
Usinsk 24G3
Usk 15E7
Üsküdar 21M4
Usman' 23H5
Usol'ye-Sibirskoye 25L4
Ussel 18F4
Ussuriysk 30C4
Ust'-Donetskiy 23I7
Ust'-Dzheguta 23I7
Ust'-Ilimsk 25L4
Ústí nad Labem 13O5
Ust'-Kamchatsk 25R4
Ust'-Kamenogorsk 27H2
Ust'-Kulom 22L3
Ust'-Kut 25L4
Ust'-Kuyga 25O2
Ust'-Labinsk 23H7
Ust'-Maya 25O3
Ust'-Nera 25P3
Ust'-Omchug 25P3
Ust'-Ordynskiy 25L4
Ust'-Tsil'ma 22L2
Ustyurt Plateau 26E2
Ustyuzhna 22H4
Usulután 50G6
Utah *state* 46E4
Utena 11N9
Utica 48D1
Utrecht 12J4
Utrera 19D5
Utsunomiya 31E5
Uttaradit 29C6
Uttoxeter 15F6
Uusikaupunki 11L6
Uutapi 35B5
Uva 22L4
Uvalde 46H6
Uvarovo 23I6
Uvinza 35D4
Uvs Nuur *salt l.* 27I1
Uwajima 31D6
Uxbridge 15G7
Uyar 24K4
Uyo 32D4
Uyuni, Salar de *salt flat* 52E8
Uzbekistan *country* 26F2
Uzhhorod 23D6
Užice 21H3
Uzlovaya 23H5
Uzunköprü 21L4

V

Vaajakoski 10N5
Vaal *r.* 37F5
Vaasa 10L5
Vác 13Q7
Vacaria 55A5
Vacaville 49B1
Vad 22J5
Vadodara 27G4
Vadsø 10P1
Vaduz 18I3
Vágur 10□1
Vaiaku 39H2
Valday 22G4
Valdayskaya Vozvyshennost' *hills* 22G4
Valdepeñas 19E4
Val-de-Reuil 15I9
Valdés, Península *pen.* 54D6
Valdez 44D3
Valdivia 54B5
Val-d'Or 45K5
Valdosta 47K5
Valença 55D1
Valence 18G4
Valencia 19F4
Valencia 52E1
Valencia, Golfo de *g.* 19G4
Valencia de Don Juan 19D2
Valenciennes 18F1
Valera 52D2
Valjevo 21H2
Valka 11O8
Valkeakoski 11N6
Valky 23G6
Valladolid 19D3
Valladolid 50G4
Valledupar 52D1
Vallejo 49A1
Vallenar 54B3
Valletta 20F7
Valley 14C5
Valley City 46H2
Valmiera 11N8
Valozhyn 11O9
Valparaíso 54B4
Valuyki 23H6
Vammala 11M6
Van 26D3
Van, Lake *salt l.* 26D3
Vanadzor 23J8
Vancouver 44F5
Vancouver 46C2
Vancouver Island 44F5
Vandalia 47J4
Vanderbijlpark 37H4
Vanderkloof Dam *resr* 36G6
Van Diemen Gulf 40G2
Vändra 11N7
Vänern *l.* 11H7
Vänersborg 11H7
Vangaindrano 35E6
Vanimo 38E2
Vanino 30F2
Vannes 18C3
Vantaa 11N6
Vanua Levu *i.* 39H3
Vanuatu *country* 39G3
Varakļāni 11O8
Varanasi 27H4
Varangerfjorden *sea chan.* 10P1
Varaždin 20G1
Varberg 11H8
Varde 11F9
Varėna 11N9
Varese 20C2
Varginha 55B3
Varkaus 10O5
Varna 21L3
Värnamo 11I8
Várpalota 20H1
Várzea da Palma 55B2
Vaslui 21L1
Västerås 11J7
Västerhaninge 11K7
Västervik 11J8
Vasto 20F3
Vasyl'kiv 23F6
Vathy 21L6
Vatican City 20E4
Vatnajökull *ice cap* 10□2
Vatra Dornei 21K1
Vättern *l.* 11I7
Vavatenina 35E5
Vava'u Group *is* 39I3
Vavoua 32C4
Vavozh 22K4
Vawkavysk 11N10
Växjö 11I8
Vazante 55B2
Veddige 11H8
Veendam 13K4
Vejle 11F9
Velebit *mts* 20F2
Velenje 20F1
Veles 21I4
Vélez-Málaga 19D5
Velika Gorica 20G2
Velika Plana 21I2
Velikaya *r.* 11P8
Veliki Preslav 21L3
Velikiye Luki 22F4
Velikiy Novgorod 22F4
Velikiy Ustyug 22J3
Veliko Tŭrnovo 21K3
Velikoye, Ozero *l.* 23I5
Velizh 22F5
Vellore 27G5
Vel'sk 22I3
Venado Tuerto 54D4
Venceslau Bráz 55A3
Vendôme 18E3
Venev 23H5
Venezuela *country* 52E2
Venezuela, Golfo de *g.* 52D1
Vengurla 27G5
Venice 20E2
Venice 47K6
Venice, Gulf of 20E2
Vénissieux 18G4
Vennesla 11E7
Venta 11M8
Ventersdorp 37H4
Ventoux, Mont *mt.* 18G4
Ventspils 11L8
Ventura 49C3
Venus Bay 42B7
Vera 19F5
Vera 54D3
Veracruz 50E5
Vera Cruz 55A3
Veraval 27G4
Verbania 20C2
Vercelli 20C2
Vercors *reg.* 18G4
Verdalsøra 10G5
Verde *r.* 55A2
Verden (Aller) 13L4
Verdun 18G2
Vereeniging 37H4
Verkhnetulomskiy 10Q2
Verkhnevilyuysk 25N3
Verkhov'ye 23H5
Vermilion 46E1
Vermillion 47H3
Vermont *state* 48E1
Vernal 46F3
Verneuk Pan *salt pan* 36E5
Vernon 44G4
Vernon 46H5
Vero Beach 47K6
Veroia 21J4
Verona 20D2
Verona 48B3
Versailles 18F2
Vertou 18D3
Verulam 37J5
Verviers 13J5
Vesele 23G7
Veselyy 23I7
Veshenskaya 23I6
Vesoul 18H3
Vesterålsfjorden *sea chan.* 10H2
Vestfjorden *sea chan.* 10H3
Vestmannaeyjar 10□2
Vesuvius *vol.* 20F4
Ves'yegonsk 22H4
Veszprém 20G1
Vetlanda 11I8
Vetluga 22J4
Vevey 18H3
Vezirköprü 23G8
Viamao 55A5
Viana 53J4
Viana 55C3
Viana do Castelo 19B3
Vianópolis 55A2
Viareggio 20D3
Viborg 11F8
Vibo Valentia 20G5
Vic 19H3
Vicenza 20D2
Vichy 18F3
Vicksburg 47I5
Viçosa 55C3
Victoria 7
Victoria 44F5
Victoria 47H6
Victoria 54B5
Victoria 54D4
Victoria *state* 42B6
Victoria, Lake 34D4
Victoria Falls 35C5
Victoria Island 44H2
Victoria West 36F6
Victorville 49D3
Videle 21K2
Viedma 54D6
Viedma, Lago *l.* 54B7
Vienna 13P6
Vienne 18G4
Vientiane 29C6
Vierzon 18F3
Viesīte 11N8
Vietnam *country* 29C6
Vigan 29E6
Vigevano 20C2
Vigia 53I4
Vignola 20D2
Vigo 19B2
Vijayawada 27H5
Vila Franca de Xira 19B4
Vilagarcía de Arousa 19B2
Vila Nova de Gaia 19B3
Vilanova i la Geltrú 19G3
Vila Real 19C3
Vilar Formoso 19C3
Vila Velha 55C3
Vil'gort 22K3
Vilhena 52F6
Viljandi 11N7
Vilkaviškis 11M9
Vilkija 11M9
Villa Ángela 54D3
Villach 13N7
Villa Dolores 54C4
Villaguay 54E4
Villahermosa 50F5
Villa Insurgentes 46E6
Villajoyosa-La Vila Joíosa 19F4
Villa María 54D4
Villa Montes 52F8
Villanueva de la Serena 19D4
Villa Ocampo 54E3
Villa Regina 54C5
Villarrica 54E3
Villarrobledo 19E4
Villa San Giovanni 20F5
Villa Unión 46G7
Villavicencio 52D3
Villazon 52E8
Villefranche-sur-Saône 18G4
Villena 19F4
Villeneuve-sur-Lot 18E4
Villers-sur-Mer 15G9
Villeurbanne 18G4
Villingen 13L6
Vilnius 11N9
Vil'nyans'k 23G7
Vilyeyka 11O9
Vilyuy *r.* 25N3
Vimmerby 11I8
Viña del Mar 54B4
Vinaròs 19G3
Vincennes 47J4
Vinchina 54C3
Vineland 48D3
Vinh 29C6
Vinita 47H4
Vinnytsya 23F6
Vinson Massif *mt.* 56C4
Vire 18D2
Virgem da Lapa 55C2
Virginia 37H5
Virginia *state* 48B4
Virginia Beach 48D4
Virgin Islands (U.K.) *terr.* 51L5
Virgin Islands (U.S.A.) *terr.* 51L5
Virginópolis 55C2
Virovitica 20G2
Visaginas 11O9
Visalia 49C2
Visby 11K8
Viscount Melville Sound *sea chan.* 45G2
Viseu 19C3
Viseu 53I4
Vishakhapatnam 27H5
Visp 18H3
Vista 49D4
Vistula *r.* 13Q3
Viterbo 20E3
Vitigudino 19C3
Viti Levu *i.* 39H3
Vitória 55C3
Vitória da Conquista 55C1
Vitoria-Gasteiz 19E2
Vitry-le-François 18G2
Vitsyebsk 23F5
Vittel 18G2
Vittoria 20F6
Vittorio Veneto 20E2
Vize 21L4
Vizianagaram 27H5
Vizinga 22K3
Vlaardingen 12J5
Vladikavkaz 23J8
Vladimir 22I4
Vladimiro-Aleksandrovskoye 30D4
Vladivostok 30C4
Vlasotince 21J3
Vlissingen 12I5
Vlorë 21H4
Vöcklabruck 13N6
Voghera 20C2
Vohipeno 35E6
Voinjama 32C4
Vojens 11F9
Vojvodina *prov.* 21H2
Vokhma 22J4
Volcano Islands 28G5
Volda 10E5
Volga 22H4
Volga *r.* 23J7
Volgodonsk 23I7
Volgograd 23J6
Volgogradskoye Vodokhranilishche *resr* 23J6
Völkermarkt 13O7
Volkhov 22G4
Vol'no-Nadezhdinskoye 30C4
Volnovakha 23H7
Volochys'k 23E6
Volodars'ke 23H7
Volodymyr-Volyns'kyy 23E6
Vologda 22H4
Volokolamsk 22G4
Volos 21J5
Volosovo 11P7
Vol'sk 23J5
Volta, Lake *resr* 32D4
Volta Redonda 55B3
Volzhsk 22K5
Volzhskiy 23J6
Vopnafjörður *b.* 10□2
Voranava 11N9
Voreies Sporades *is* 21J5
Vorkuta 24H3
Voronezh 23H6
Vorotynets 22J4
Võru 11O8
Vosburg 36F6
Vosges *mts* 18H3
Voskresensk 23H5
Voss 11E6
Vostochnyy Sayan *mts* 25K4
Votkinsk 24G4
Votuporanga 55A3
Vozhega 22I3
Voznesens'k 23F7
Vrangel' 30D4
Vranje 21I3
Vratsa 21J3
Vrbas 21H2
Vredenburg 36C7
Vršac 21I2
Vryburg 36G4
Vryheid 37J4
Vsevolozhsk 22F3
Vukovar 21H2
Vuktyl' 24G3
Vukuzakhe 37I4
Vurnary 22J5
Vushtrri 21I3
Vyatskiye Polyany 22K4
Vyazemskiy 30D3
Vyaz'ma 23G5
Vyazniki 22I4
Vyborg 11P6
Vychegda *r.* 22J3
Vyerkhnyadzvinsk 11O9
Vyksa 23I5
Vynohradiv 23D6
Vyselki 23H7
Vyshhorod 23F6
Vyshniy-Volochek 22G4
Vyškov 13P6
Vytegra 22H3

W

Wa 32C3
Waco 47H5
Waddeneilanden 12J4
Waddenzee *sea chan.* 12J4
Wadi Halfa 33G2
Wad Medani 33G3
Wagga Wagga 42C5
Wahpeton 47H2
Waidhofen an der Ybbs 13O7
Wajima 31E5
Wakatipu, Lake 43B7
Wakayama 31D6
Wakefield 14F5
Wakkanai 30F3
Wałbrzych 13P5
Walcha 42E3
Wałcz 13P4
Waldkraiburg 13N6
Waldorf 48C3
Wales *admin. div.* 15D6
Walgett 42D3
Walkersville 48C3
Wallasey 14D5
Walla Walla 46D2
Wallis and Futuna Islands *terr.* 39I3
Walnut Creek 49A2
Walsall 15F6
Walterboro 47K5
Waltham 48F1
Walvis Bay 36B2
Walvis Bay 36B2
Wamba 32D4
Wamba 34C3
Wanaka, Lake 43B7
Wanganui 43E4
Wangaratta 42C6
Wangkui 30B3
Wangqing 30C4
Wantage 15F7
Wanxian 27J3
Wanyuan 27J3
Warab 33F4
Warangal 27G5
Waren 13N4
Warendorf 13K5
Warialda 42E2
Warmbad 36D5
Warminster 15E7
Warminster 48D2
Warracknabeal 41I7
Warrego *r.* 42B3
Warren 42C3
Warren 48A2
Warren 48B2
Warrenpoint 17F3
Warrensburg 47I4
Warri 32D4
Warrington 14E5
Warrnambool 41I7
Warsaw 13R4
Warwick 15F6
Warwick 42F2
Warwick 48F2
Wasco 49C3
Washington 47L4
Washington 48A2
Washington 48C3
Washington *state* 46C2
Washington, Mount 47M3
Watampone 29E8
Waterbury 48E2
Waterford 17E5
Waterford Harbour 17F5
Waterloo 47I3
Waterloo 48A1
Waterloo 48C1
Waterlooville 15F8
Watertown 47H3
Watertown 47L3
Waterval Boven 37J3
Watford 15G7
Watsonville 49B2
Wau 33F4
Wauchope 42F3
Waukegan 47J3
Wausau 47J3
Waverly 48C1
Waycross 47K5
Waynesboro 48B3
Wear *r.* 14F4
Weatherford 46H5
Webi Shabeelle *r.* 34E3
Webster 48F1
Weddell Sea 56C5
Wee Waa 42D3
Weifang 27K3
Weimar 13M5
Weinan 27J3
Weipa 41I2
Weirton 48A2
Weiz 13O7
Wejherowo 13Q3
Weldiya 34D2
Welkom 37H4
Welland 48B1
Wellesley Islands 41H3
Wellingborough 15G6
Wellington 36D7
Wellington 43E5
Wells-next-the-Sea 15H6
Wels 13O6
Welwyn Garden City 15G7
Wembesi 37I5
Wenatchee 46C2
Wenshan 27J4
Wenzhou 28E5
Werris Creek 42E3
Wesel 13K5
Wesselton 37I4
West Bank *terr.* 33G1
West Bend 47J3
West Bromwich 15F6
Westbury 15E7
West Chester 48D3
Westerly 48F2
Western Australia *state* 40E4
Western Cape *prov.* 36E7
Western Desert 33F2
Western Ghats *mts* 27G5
Western Port *b.* 42B7
Western Sahara *terr.* 32B2
West Falkland *i.* 54D8
Westfield 48E1
West Hartford 48E2
West Haven 48E2
West Indies *is* 51J4
Westminster 48C3
Weston-super-Mare 15E7
West Palm Beach 47K6
West Plains 47I4
West Point 48C4
Westray *i.* 16F1
Westray Firth *sea chan.* 16F1
West Siberian Plain 24J3
West Virginia *state* 48A3
West Wyalong 42C4
West York 48C3
Wete 35D4
Wetzlar 13L5
Wewak 38E2
Wexford 17F5
Weybridge 15G7
Weyburn 44H5
Weymouth 15E8
Weymouth 48F1
Whalsay *i.* 16□
Whangarei 43E2
Wharton 47H6
Wheaton-Glenmont 48C3
Wheeling 48A2
Whernside *hill* 14E4
Whitburn 16F5
Whitby 14G4
Whitehaven 14D4
Whitehead 17G3
Whitehill 15G7
Whitehorse 44E3
White Nile *r.* 33G3
White Plains 48E2
White Sea 22H2
Whiteville 47L5
White Volta *r.* 32C4
Whitley Bay 14F3
Whitney, Mount 49C2
Whitstable 15I7
Whittlesea 42B6
Whittlesey 15G6
Whyalla 41H6
Wichita 47H4
Wichita Falls 46H5
Wick 16F2
Wickford 15H7
Wicklow 17F5
Wicklow Head 17G5
Wicklow Mountains 17F5
Widnes 14E5
Wieluń 13Q5
Wiener Neustadt 13P7
Wiesbaden 13L5
Wigan 14E5
Wight, Isle of *i.* 15F8
Wigston 15F6
Wigtown Bay 16E6
Wild Coast 37I6
Wilge *r.* 37I3
Wilhelm, Mount 38E2
Wilhelmshaven 13L4
Wilkes-Barre 48D2
Wilkes Land *reg.* 56A5
Willand 15D8
Willemstad 51K6
Williamsburg 48C4
Williams Lake 44F4
Williamsport 48C2
Williamstown 48D1
Williamstown 48D3
Willimantic 48E2
Williston 46G2
Williston Lake 44F4
Willmar 47H2
Wilmington 47L5
Wilmington 48D3
Wilmslow 14E5
Wilson 47L4
Wilson's Promontory *pen.* 42C7
Wincanton 15E7
Winchester 15F7
Winchester 47K4
Winchester 48B3
Windber 48B2
Windermere 14E4
Windermere *l.* 14E4
Windhoek 36C2
Windsor 15G7
Windsor 42E4
Windsor 45J5
Windsor Locks 48E2
Windward Islands 51L5
Windward Passage 51J5
Winfield 47H4
Wingate 14F4
Wingham 42F3
Winneba 32C4
Winnemucca 46D3
Winnfield 47I5
Winnipeg 45I5
Winnipeg, Lake 45I4
Winnipegosis, Lake 45H4
Winona 47I3
Winona 47J5
Winsford 14E5
Winston-Salem 47K4
Winterthur 18I3
Winton 41I4
Wisbech 15H6
Wisconsin *state* 47J3
Wisconsin Rapids 47J3
Wishaw 16F5
Wismar 13M4
Witbank 37I3
Witham 15H7
Witney 15F7
Wittenberge 13M4
Włocławek 13Q4
Wodonga 42C6
Woking 15G7
Wokingham 15G7
Wolfenbüttel 13M4
Wolfsberg 13O7
Wolfsburg 13M4
Wollaston Lake 44H4
Wollongong 42E5
Wolverhampton 15E6
Wondai 41K5
Wŏnju 31B5
Wŏnsan 31B5
Woodbine 48D3
Woodbridge 15I6
Woodbridge 48C3
Woodbury 48D3
Woodland 49B1
Woods, Lake of the 45I5
Woodstock 48A1
Woodward 46H4
Wooler 14E3
Woolgoolga 42F3
Woomera 41H6
Woonsocket 48F1
Wooster 47K3
Worcester 15E6
Worcester 36D7
Worcester 48F1
Workington 14D4
Worksop 14F5
Worland 46F3
Worthing 15G8
Wotu 38C2
Wrangel Island 25T2
Wrexham 15E5
Wrightwood 49D3
Wrocław 13P5
Września 13P4
Wuchang 30B3
Wuhai 27J3
Wuhan 27K3
Wuhu 28D4
Wuliang Shan *mts* 27J4
Wuppertal 13K5
Wurno 32D3
Würzburg 13L6
Wuwei 27J3
Wuxi 28E4
Wuyi Shan *mts* 28D5
Wuyuan 28C3
Wuzhong 27J3
Wuzhou 27K4
Wymondham 15I6
Wyndham 40F3
Wyndham-Werribee 42B6
Wyoming *state* 46F3
Wyszków 13R4
Wythall 15F6
Wytheville 48A4

X

Xai-Xai 37K3
Xambioa 53I5
Xam Nua 28C5
Xankändi 26D3
Xanthi 21K4
Xàtiva 19F4
Xiamen 28D5
Xi'an 27J3
Xiangfan 27K3
Xiangtan 27K4
Xianyang 27J3
Xiao Hinggan Ling *mts* 30B2
Xichang 27J4
Xifeng 30B4
Xigazê 27H4
Xi Jiang *r.* 27K4
Xilinhot 27K2
Xinglongzhen 30B3
Xingu *r.* 53H4
Xinguara 53H5
Xingyi 27J4
Xining 27J3
Xinqing 30C2
Xintai 27K3
Xinxiang 27K3
Xinyang 27K3
Xinzhou 27K3
Xique Xique 53J6
Xo'jayli 26E2
Xuddur 34E3
Xúquer, Riu *r.* 19F4
Xuwen 27K4
Xuzhou 27K3

Y

Ya'an 27J3
Yabuli 30C3
Yadrin 22J5
Yagodnoye 25P3
Yagoua 33E3
Yahualica 50D4
Yaizu 31E6
Yakima 46C2
Yako 32C3
Yakovlevka 30D3
Yakutsk 25N3
Yakymivka 23G7
Yala 29C7
Yalova 21M4
Yalta 23G7
Yalvaç 21N5
Yamagata 31F5
Yamaguchi 31C6
Yamal Peninsula 24H2
Yamba 42F2
Yambio 33F4
Yambol 21L3
Yamoussoukro 32C4
Yampil' 23F6
Yamuna *r.* 27H4
Yana *r.* 25O2
Yan'an 27J3
Yanbu' al Baḥr 34D1
Yangdok 31B5
Yangtze *r.* 27L3
Yangyang 31C5
Yanji 30C4
Yankton 47H3
Yantai 28E4
Yaoundé 32E4
Yap *i.* 29F7
Yaqui *r.* 46E6
Yar 22L4
Yaransk 22J4
Yaren 39G2
Yarīm 34E2
Yaroslavl' 22H4
Yaroslavskiy 30D3
Yarra Junction 42B6
Yarram 42C7
Yarrawonga 42B6
Yartsevo 23G5
Yashkul' 23J7
Yasnogorsk 23H5
Yass 42D5
Yatağan 21M6
Yatsushiro 31C6
Yavari *r.* 52E4
Yavoriv 23D6
Yazd 26E3
Yazoo City 47I5
Ydra *i.* 21J6
Yefremov 23H5
Yegorlykskaya 23I7
Yegor'yevsk 23H5
Yekaterinburg 24H4
Yekaterinoslavka 30C2
Yelabuga 22K5
Yelan' 23I6
Yelets 23H5
Yell *i.* 16□
Yellowknife 44G3
Yellow *r.* 27K3
Yellow Sea 28E4
Yell Sound *strait* 16□
Yel'sk 23F6
Yemen *country* 34E2
Yemtsa 22I3
Yemva 22K3
Yenagoa 32D4
Yenakiyeve 23H6
Yenice 21L5
Yenişehir 21M4
Yenisey *r.* 24J2
Yeniseysk 24K4
Yeniseyskiy Kryazh *ridge* 24K4
Yenotayevka 23J7
Yeovil 15E8
Yeppoon 41K4
Yerevan 26D2
Yereymentau 27G1
Yergeni *hills* 23J7
Yershov 23K6
Yertsevo 22I3
Yesan 31B5
Yesil' 26F1
Yeşilova 21M6
Yessentuki 23I7
Yevlax 23J8
Yevpatoriya 23G7
Yevreyskaya Avtonomnaya Oblast' *admin. div.* 30D2
Yeysk 23H7
Yi'an 30B3
Yibin 27J4
Yichun 30C3
Yilan 30C3
Yimianpo 30C3
Yinchuan 27J3
Yingkou 27L2
Yingtan 28D5
Yining 27H2
Yirga Alem 34D3
Yitulihe 30A2
Yiyang 27K4
Ylivieska 10N4
Ylöjärvi 11M6
Yogyakarta 29D8
Yokadouma 33E4
Yokkaichi 31E6
Yoko 32E4
Yokohama 31E6
Yokosuka 31E6
Yokote 31F5
Yola 32E4
Yŏnan 31B5
Yonezawa 31F5
Yong'an 28D5
Yŏnghŭng 31B5
Yŏngju 31C5
Yonkers 48E2
Yopal 52D2
York 14F5
York 48B1
York 48C3
York, Cape 41I2
Yorke Peninsula 41H7
Yorkshire Wolds *hills* 14G5
Yorkton 44H4
Yoshkar-Ola 22J4
Youghal 17E6
Youngstown 48A2
Yozgat 26C3
Yreka 46C3
Ystad 11H9
Ysyk-Köl *salt l.* 27G2
Ytyk-Kyuyel' 25O3
Yuba City 49B1
Yucatán *pen.* 50F5
Yucatan Channel *strait* 51G4
Yucca Valley 49D3
Yueyang 27K4
Yukon *r.* 44B3
Yukon Territory *admin. div.* 44E3
Yulin 27K4
Yuma 49E4
Yumen 27I3
Yungas *reg.* 52E7
Yurga 24J4
Yuriria 50D4
Yur'ya 22K4
Yur'yevets 22I4
Yur'yev-Pol'skiy 22H4
Yushu 27I3
Yushu 30B3
Yuxi 27J4
Yuzawa 31F5
Yuzha 22I4
Yuzhno-Kuril'sk 30G3
Yuzhno-Sakhalinsk 30F3
Yuzhno-Sukhokumsk 23J7
Yuzhnoukrayinsk 23F7
Yverdon 18H3

Z

Zaandam 12J4
Zabaykal'sk 27K2
Zabīd 34E2
Zābol 26F3
Zacapa 50G5
Zacatecas 50D4
Zacharo 21I6
Zacoalco 50D4
Zadar 20F2
Zadonsk 23H5
Zafra 19C4
Zaghouan 20D6
Zagreb 20F2
Zagros Mountains 26E3
Zāhedān 26F4
Zahlé 33G1
Ẓahrān 34E2
Zaječar 21J3
Zākhō 33H1
Zakopane 13Q6
Zakynthos 21I6
Zakynthos *i.* 21I6
Zalaegerszeg 20G1
Zalai-domsag *hills* 20G1
Zalantun 30A3
Zalău 21J1
Ẓalim 34E1
Zambezi *r.* 35C5
Zambia *country* 35C5
Zamboanga 29E7
Zamora 19D3
Zamora 52C4
Zamora de Hidalgo 50D5
Zamość 23D6
Zanesville 47K4
Zanjān 33H1
Zanzibar 35D4
Zanzibar Island 35D4
Zaozernyy 25K4
Zaozhuang 27K3
Zapadnaya Dvina 22G4
Zapadnyy Kazakhstan *admin. div.* 23K6
Zapadnyy Sayan *reg.* 24J4
Zapata 46H6
Zapolyarnyy 10Q2
Zaporizhzhya 23G7
Zaqatala 23J8
Zaragoza 19F3
Zarand 26E3
Zaranj 26F3
Zarasai 11O9
Zárate 54E4
Zaraysk 23H5
Zaraza 52E2
Zärdab 23J8
Zaria 32D3
Zarichne 23E6
Zărnești 21K2
Żary 13O5
Zavetnoye 23I7
Zavidoviči 20H2
Zavitinsk 30C2
Zavolzhsk 22I4
Zawiercie 13Q5
Zaysan, Lake 27H2
Žďar nad Sázavou 13O6
Zdolbuniv 23E6
Zeerust 37H3
Zeil, Mount 40G4
Zelenodol'sk 22K5
Zelenograd 22H4
Zelenogradsk 11L9
Zelenokumsk 23I7
Zell am See 13N7
Zemetchino 23I5
Zemmora 19G6
Zenica 20G2
Zenzach 19H6
Zernograd 23I7
Zeya 30B1
Zgierz 13Q5
Zhabinka 11N10
Zhanaozen 26E2
Zhangjiakou 27K2
Zhangye 27J3
Zhanibek 23J6
Zhanjiang 27K4
Zhaodong 30B3
Zhaotong 27J4
Zhaoyuan 30B3
Zhaozhou 30B3
Zharkent 27H2
Zharkovskiy 22G5
Zhashkiv 23F6
Zheleznogorsk 23G5
Zhengzhou 27K3
Zhenlai 30A3
Zherdevka 23I6
Zhezkazgan 26F2
Zhitikara 26F1
Zhlobin 23F5
Zhmerynka 23F6
Zhob 27F3
Zhongwei 27J3
Zhovti Vody 23G6
Zhuanghe 31A5
Zhukovka 23G5
Zhukovskiy 23H5
Zhuzhou 27K4
Zhydachiv 23E6
Zhytkavichy 11O10
Zhytomyr 23F6
Žiar nad Hronom 13Q6
Zibo 27K3
Zielona Góra 13O5
Zigong 27J4
Ziguinchor 32B3
Žilina 13Q6
Zima 25L4
Zimbabwe *country* 35C5
Zimnicea 21K3
Zimovniki 23I7
Zinder 32D3
Ziniaré 32C3
Zinjibār 34E2
Zirc 20G1
Zitácuaro 50D5
Zittau 13O5
Zlín 13P6
Zmiyevka 23H5
Znamenka 23I5
Znam"yanka 23G6
Znojmo 13P6
Zolochiv 23E6
Zolochiv 23G6
Zolotonosha 23G6
Zolotukhino 23H5
Zomba 35D5
Zongo 34B3
Zonguldak 21N4
Zorgho 32C3
Żory 13Q5
Zouérat 32B2
Zrenjanin 21I2
Zubova Polyana 23I5
Zubtsov 22G4
Zuénoula 32C4
Zug 18I3
Zugdidi 23I8
Zunyi 27J4
Županja 20H2
Zürich 18I3
Zuru 32D3
Zuwārah 32E1
Zuyevka 22K4
Zvishavane 35D6
Zvolen 13Q6
Zwedru 32C4
Zwelitsha 37H7
Zwettl 13O6
Zwickau 13N5
Zwolle 13K4
Zyryanka 25Q3

Collins Canadian World Atlas

An imprint of HarperCollins Publishers
2 Bloor St. E., 20th Floor
Toronto, Ontario
M4W 1A8

First Published 1986
Second Edition 1991
Third Edition 1993
Fourth Edition 1994
Fifth Edition 1997
Sixth Edition 2003
Seventh Edition 2005
Eighth Edition 2007
Ninth Edition 2009

First Canadian Edition 2003
Second Canadian Edition 2009, reprinted 2010

Copyright © HarperCollins Publishers 2009

Maps © Collins Bartholomew Ltd 2009

Collins ® is a registered trademark of HarperCollins Publishers Ltd

All rights reserved. No part of this publication may be reproduced, stored in a retrieval system, or transmitted, in any form or by any means, electronic, mechanical, photocopying, recording or otherwise without the prior written permission of the publisher and copyright owners.

The contents of this edition of the Collins Canadian World Atlas are believed correct at the time of printing. Nevertheless the publisher can accept no responsibility for errors or omissions, changes in the detail given, or for any expense or loss thereby caused.

Printed in Hong Kong

British Library Cataloguing in Publication Data.
A catalogue record for this book is available from the British Library.

ISBN 978-0-00-784731-0

Imp002

All mapping in this atlas is generated from Collins Bartholomew™ digital databases. Collins Bartholomew™, the UK's leading independent geographical information supplier, can provide a digital, custom, and premium mapping service to a variety of markets. For further information:

Tel: +44 (0) 141 306 3752
e-mail: collinsbartholomew@harpercollins.co.uk

We also offer a choice of books, atlases and maps that can be customized to suit a customer's own requirements. For further information:

Tel: +44 (0) 1242 258155
e-mail: business.gifts@harpercollins.co.uk
or visit our website at: www.collinsbartholomew.com

Cover image: Blue Marble: Next Generation. NASA's Earth Observatory

Easy reference atlas to help you discover every corner of the globe

Discover Canada – detailed mapping of Canada

Explore the whole world – accurate and up-to-date maps of every corner of the world

Know the facts – ranking tables of the world's top 20 major geographical features plus flags and statistics on every country of the world

Find that place – over 10 000 places mapped and indexed

BELIZE		22 965	8 867	288 000	Belmopan	English, Spanish, Mayan, creole
CANADA		9 984 670	3 855 103	32 876 000	Ottawa	English, French, local languages
COSTA RICA		51 100	19 730	4 468 000	San José	Spanish
CUBA		110 860	42 803	11 268 000	Havana	Spanish
DOMINICA		750	290	67 000	Roseau	English, creole
DOMINICAN REPUBLIC		48 442	18 704	9 760 000	Santo Domingo	Spanish, creole
EL SALVADOR		21 041	8 124	6 857 000	San Salvador	Spanish
GRENADA		378	146	106 000	St George's	English, creole	Roman Catholic, Protestant
GUATEMALA		108 890	42 043	13 354 000	Guatemala City	Spanish, Mayan languages	Roman Catholic, Protestant
HAITI		27 750	10 714	9 598 000	Port-au-Prince	French, creole	Roman Catholic, Protestant, Voodoo
HONDURAS		112 088	43 277	7 106 000	Tegucigalpa	Spanish, Amerindian languages	Roman Catholic, Protestant
JAMAICA		10 991	4 244	2 714 000	Kingston	English, creole	Protestant, Roman Catholic
MEXICO		1 972 545	761 604	106 535 000	Mexico City	Spanish, Amerindian languages	Roman Catholic, Protestant
NICARAGUA		130 000	50 193	5 603 000	Managua	Spanish, Amerindian languages	Roman Catholic, Protestant
PANAMA		77 082	29 762	3 343 000	Panama City	Spanish, English, Amerindian languages	Roman Catholic, Protestant, Sunni Muslim
ST KITTS AND NEVIS		261	101	50 000	Basseterre	English, creole	Protestant, Roman Catholic
LUCIA		616	238	165 000	Castries	English, creole	Roman Catholic, Protestant

CAN $1

ISBN 978-0-0

9 780007 847310

www.harpercollins.ca

G is for glaciers
That used to abound
Till we screwed up the climate
That kept them around.

H is for horsemen,
Far more now than four.
Clippitty, clopitty,
Soon at your door.

J is for judgment,
A voice from on high,
Sending sinners to hell
As they weep, wail, and cry.

O is for oceans
Expanding and hot.
Reefs bleaching, whales beaching,
Fish living? Guess not!

R is for robots,
Increasingly smart.
They'll figure us out
And then rip us apart.

S is for scarcity of
Food, air, and water.
Share the last Twinkie
On Earth with your daughter.

W's for weirdness
Afflicting the weather.
Broiling or drowning,
We'll all die together.

X is for extinction.
As more species die,
Humans will follow—
There's no time to cry.

Z is for zombies
That come in the night
And hide in your closet—
Don't turn out the light!

Paul Lewis

Paul Lewis is an English professor at Boston College, the president of the Poe Studies Association, and the author of *Cracking Up: American Humor in a Time of Conflict*. A fascination with gothic fiction and horror films prepared him to publish "The Funeral Game" in *Crazy Magazine* while he was in graduate school, coin the word "Frankenfood" at the dawn of the GMO era, and write *A Is for Asteroids, Z Is for Zombies* as gallows humor for a time of global threats. While we need, perhaps desperately, to take these threats seriously, we also need to find relief from the anxiety they provoke. In this spirit, Lewis asks, "If you can't laugh about the Apocalypse, what can you laugh about?"

Kenneth Lamug

Ken Lamug is an author and illustrator best known for his award-winning children's book *A Box Story*, an adult humor book *Hurts Like a Mother: A Cautionary Alphabet*, and the macabre fairy tale *The Stumps of Flattop Hill*. He also created the graphic adventure *The Tall Tales of Talbot Toluca* and is the cocreator of the steampunk comic series *Monstrous*. You can see more of his work at www.RabbleBoy.com.

Andrews McMeel Publishing
a division of Andrews McMeel Universal
1130 Walnut Street, Kansas City, Missouri 64106

www.andrewsmcmeel.com

17 18 19 20 21 TEN 10 9 8 7 6 5 4 3 2 1

ISBN: 978-1-4494-8688-4

Editor: Patty Rice
Designer: Spencer Williams
Art Director: Tim Lynch
Production Editor: Erika Kuster
Production Manager: Tamara Haus

ATTENTION: SCHOOLS AND BUSINESSES

Andrews McMeel books are available at quantity discounts with bulk purchase for educational, business, or sales promotional use. For information, please e-mail the Andrews McMeel Publishing Special Sales Department: specialsales@amuniversal.com.